Indian Drama Today

A Study in the Theme of Cultural Deformity

In the same series

New Directions in Indian Drama
Sudhakar Pandey and Freya Barua, ed.

Studies in Contemporary Indian Drama
Sudhakar Pandey and Freya Taraporewala, ed.

Indian Drama Today

A Study in the Theme of Cultural Deformity

Manchi Sarat Babu

PRESTIGE

Published by
Prestige Books
3/28, East Patel Nagar
New Delhi 110 008

ISBN: 81-7551-026-9

1997

Photo Typesetting by
Pivot Computers
Delhi 110 006
Ph. 293 4490

Printed at
Mehra Offset Press
New Delhi 110 002

Contents

Dedicated to

Hymavathi, mother

Venkatanarasaiah, father

Dr. V. Krishna Murthy, M.D., friend

Vijayalakshmi, wife

and

Prof. K. Venkata Reddy, Ph.D., guru

to whom I owe what I'm able

to achieve here

Acknowledgements

I am immensely indebted to Prof. K. Venkata Reddy, my research supervisor who has carved a research scholar in me and who has always encouraged me affectionately. I am very grateful to Prof. V. Rangan of Nagarajuna University for initiating me into research work and affectionately steering me in a right path. I am very thankful to Dr. P. Obula Reddy for proof-reading my thesis patiently and giving suggestions. And I owe the successful completion of my thesis to Dr. P. Sudhakar who has patiently and affectionately taken all the trouble for my sake.

I am greatly obliged to Mr. Girish Karnad, Mr. Badal Sircar, Mr. Shriram Lagoo and Mr. Vijay Tendulkar for sparing their valuable time for me and clarifying my doubts.

I express my profound gratitude to:

Dr R.K. Dhawan of Delhi University, Dr P. Purnachandra Rao of Ethnic Arts Centre, Hyd. and Prof. Prashant Sinha of Pune University for their suggestions and co-operation.

The librarians and staff of S.K. University Library, Nagarjuna University Library, S.R. Library of Guntur, University of Hyderabad Library, Ramesh Mohan Library of CIEFL, ASRC Library, Osmania University Library and Kakatiya University Library, especially to Prof. L.S. Ramaiah, Mr. Jagga Rao, Mr. A. Somaiah of CIEFL, Mr. Sarat Babu of Nagarjuna University, Mrs. E. Renuka of Kakatiya University, Mr. R.R. Joseph and Mr. K. Saratchandra Babu of Jawahar Bharati, Kavali and Ms. M. Vijaya Lakshmi of Sahitya Akademi for helping me greatly in getting the relevant material for my work,

My friends and colleagues Dr. G.S. Venugopal, Mr. G. Shantivardhan, Mr. B. Krupakar, and Mr. K.V. Muthyam of Anantapur, Dr. M.A. Obaiah, Mr. K.R.K. Murthy of Kavali, Mr. C. Koteswara Rao, Dr. P. Chenna Reddy, Dr. C. B.C. Mohan and Mr. J. Ravindranath for their friendly help and encouragement and Mr. V. Chiranjeevachari, for his brotherly help and co-operation,

Prestige Books for bringing out this book beautifully,

Mrs. S. Vahini, Mrs. R. Jyothi my sisters, Mr. M. Ravi my brother, Ms. V. Nirmala Devi, my niece, Mr. Y. Vachaspati, my nephew, Ms. M. Athena, Mr. M. Plato my children and many other kin and friends for helping and encouraging me in many ways.

Preface

Like Indian English Drama, Indian Drama in English translation has not received the critical attention that it deserves. The only book—*Modern Indian Drama in English Translation* by Veena Noble Dass—so far produced, is a general study of the post-Independence Indian Drama translated into English.

The present book aims at making in-depth study of the theme of cultural deformity in its variegated aspects as revealed in the plays of Mohan Rakesh, Girish Karnad, Vijay Tendulkar and Badal Sircar translated into English. It adopts certain concepts of Transactional Analysis, originated by Dr. Eric Berne and developed by Claude M. Steiner with a view to gaining fresh insights into the plays under study.

Culture suppresses human nature and distorts human personality in six ways according to Claude M. Steiner. This reflects in six kinds of cultural deformity as can be seen. If maleness and femaleness are biologically determined, masculinity and feminity are culturally programmed. Consequently, men become masculine and women, feminine whereby they acquire incomplete personalities, leading to gender deformity. In India, people are divided into various castes and classes which are hierarchized. This results in the inhuman exploitation and oppression of one by another, thereby causing social deformity. As people take hierarchies for granted, they give away their power and become powerless. So they play power games to overcome their acquired powerlessness, manifesting political deformity. The division and hierarchization of the society bring about the alienation of the mind from the body in individuals, resulting in physical deformity. So, people find life joyless and meaningless, and in order to overcome their joylessness and meaninglessness of their lives, they become addicted to liquor, loveless sex, religious perversion and idealism. Religion, éducation and mass media, polluted by political and commercial interests, make people mindless, subjecting them to mental deformity which sustains other deformities of culture. The mad scramble to reach the top in the hierarchized society dehumanizes people and makes them loveless, culminating in spiritual deformity. These six deformities form a kind of cultural labyrinth in which modern men and women are trapped.

An attempt is made in the present work to show how these cultural deformities—gender, social, political, physical, mental and spiritual—are treated in the select plays of Mohan Rakesh, Girish Karnad, Vijay Tendulkar and Badal Sircar, translated into English. The book is divided into eight chapters. The first chapter briefly explains the cultural deformity of Indian society, shows how it is treated in Indian English Drama of pre- and post-Independence periods and gives a short introduction to the chosen playwrights. The second chapter deals with gender deformity in Tendulkar's *Kamala*, Karnad's *Naga-Mandala* and Rakesh's *Half-Way House,* and shows how both men and women suffer on account of gender deformity though women suffer more than men in our patriarchal society. The third chapter examines social deformity in Karnad's *Tale-Danda*, Sircar's *Stale News* and Rakesh's *One Day in Ashadha*, and traces its evil effects in social and economic spheres and its resilience in surviving revolutions. The fourth chapter probes into political deformity in Karnad's *Tughlaq,* Tendulkar's *Ghasiram Kotwal* and Sircar's *That Other History*, and elucidates the roles that people play in their struggle for power. The fifth chapter analyses physical deformity in Karnad's *Hayavadana*, Tendulkar's *Sakharam Binder* and Sircar's *Evam Indrajit,* and finds how people become perverted to overcome its evil effects. The sixth chapter traces mental deformity in Sircar's *Procession* and Tendulkar's *Encounter in Umbugland* and *Kanyadan*, and shows how people are made mindless in various ways. The seventh chapter explores spiritual deformity in Rakesh's *The Great Swans of the Waves*, Sircar's *Bhoma* and Tendulkar's *The Vultures*, and thus illustrates the causes and effects of spiritual deformity. The last chapter summarizes the argument and draws certain conclusions.

Introductory

. . . man is by nature good, and the acts and institutions of civilization have produced perverted expression of his true nature.

Rousseau

. . . All the world's a stage
And all the men and women merely players.

Shakespeare

These two epigraphs succinctly but aptly describe the human condition as it obtains today. Human beings, who are not living a full-blooded life, but only existing, seem to play various roles which are culturally attributed to them. In doing so, they get alienated from their real nature. This seems to be the basic cause for all the problems that they have been facing since the dawn of civilization. And drama truly reflects the cultural deformity of human life more than any other genre of literature does.

Human beings feel proud of their culture and civilization which they have evolved through ages of their tireless endeavour. But, they are not really happy in as much as the milk of human nature is sapped by culture and civilization. They have constructed their own world, based on their acquired culture and civilization, in order to overcome and compensate for their biological inadequancies, as maintained by Peter L. Berger.[1] This has involved the processes of division, differentiation, alienation and antagonism which both the individual and the society have undergone. While discussing the Indian concept of creation, J. Bruce Long points out: "In more specific terms, it might be said that the act of fragmenting the primal unity and distributing the parts throughout the world along lines of bi-polar opposition, was both a necessary precondition for the emergence of the world-order and a tragic testimony to the world's imperfection."[2]

The fragmentation of the primal unity is endorsed by Indian dramatists like Badal Sircar and Mohan Rakesh. Sircar aptly observes: "I am a fragmented man living in a fragmented world full of contradictions."[3] Mohan Rakesh shares the same mood:

> Everyone of us is living a life in fragments. During the course of one single day one is forced to play ten different parts and some times more than one version of each part. What remains constant is one's sense of being: the idea of a crisis. It is this that I call today's mood of life. And it is in this sense that one feels fragmented . . . something like an atomic fission keeps taking place in the landscape of one's mind.[4]

While some fragments overdevelop, others remain underdeveloped according to the dictates of culture. For example, an intellectual develops his mind and neglects his body whereas a worker develops his body and neglects his mind. This uneven growth makes man incomplete and deformed. Devadatta, an intellectual, and Kapila, an athlete, suffer from this incompleteness and deformity in Girish Karnad's *Hayavadana*. In his agony, Kapila questions: "Why should one tolerate this mad dance of incompleteness?"[5] So, in the process of culture and civilization, man has become fragmented, deformed and dehumanized as Marx described him.[6]

Division of labour is a product of culture and civilization. It generates certain roles which become canonized. The human world of culture and civilization creates new needs which also bring about some new roles. Everybody plays a number of roles. People are neither good nor bad, but are considered good in certain roles and bad in certain other roles. Both the roles of a cop and a thief are created by civilization and canonized by culture. A person playing the role of cop need not be completely good and a person playing the role of a thief need not be absolutely bad. The same person can be good in a certain role and bad in another. Vijay Tendulkar, talking about his characters, says:

> A violent goonda may be equally noble at heart, a smuggler extremely god-fearing and religious, a popular chief minister may be a sex-maniac, an affectionate and loving father may be corrupt as a public servant, a brilliant poet may be a rank opportunist, 'Good' is invariably entangled with 'bad' . . .[7]

Anthropological studies prove that criminal behaviour of the people is also a product of culture. Gamst and Norbeck observe:

> Criminals, alcoholics, sexual deviants, drug addicts and juvenile delinquents are seen primarily as 'the products of society,' that is

> as the result of certain combinations of cultural factors with unintended effects upon human life. Studies of socially normal types of personality conducted by all fields of the social sciences similarly tend strongly to reflect the anthropological view that personality is largely a mirror of culture.

One's personality is a complex product of the interaction of various roles that one has to play. People are trained in playing these culturally programmed roles from their birth. They grow deformed and dehumanized as they learn playing their roles.

Certain concepts of Transactional Analysis, a post-Freudian school of psychology, originated by Dr Eric Berne, are made use of in defining and describing various deformities that form our culture. Claude M. Steiner, an intimate friend and disciple of Eric Berne, in his brilliant book, *Scripts People Live*, discusses six basic maladies of our culture: Sex role scripting, inequality, powerlessness, joylessness, mindlessness and lovelessness. These observations of Steiner facilitated the derivation of a paradigm to study the cultural milieu of Indian society.

The six basic maladies of our culture generate six kinds of deformities. Each deformity influences and reinforces the other. All the six deformities form a powerful, effective, resilient network. This network of deformities forms the cultural labyrinth where people get lost. They hardly perceive the real cause of their various problems. When they try to solve a problem, they get entangled in other problems. In their strife, they become exhausted and accept the oppressive life style. This is because when one deformity is attacked, it is unitedly saved by the other deformities from danger. Therefore, revolutions that aim at destroying one or a few deformities inevitably fail and effect costume changes only. A brief study of the six deformities will elucidate the paradigm of cultural labyrinth.

By nature, human beings are neither masculine nor feminine. Men become masculine by suppressing their potential for nurturing and intuition while women become feminine by suppressing their potential for controlling and rationality. In obeying the sexist culture, both men and women suppress their potential for spontaneity. This is done by the sexist cultural environment which inscribes firmly sex roles on the tender minds of children. So, children grow into masculine men and feminine women and acquire deformed personalities.[9] This is gender deformity. It deprives both men and women of the real joy of life. But women suffer more than men in our patriarchal society.

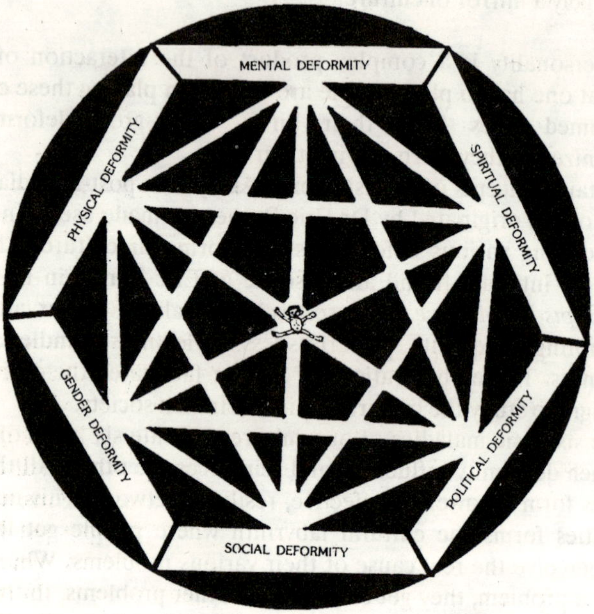

A LABYRINTH OF CULTURAL DEFORMITIES

Division of labour based on the nature of work breaks human society into several fragments. In course of socio-cultural evolution, these divisions become hierarchized, resulting in inequality. In Hindu society, the social inequality took the form of caste system.[10] The people of lower castes toil and produce wealth which the people of higher castes enjoy. Socio-econonic inequality has co-existed with and influenced socio-cultural inequality greatly. Consequently, the poor of even a higher caste suffer illtreatment and humiliation at the hands of the rich of their own caste while the condition of the poor of a lower caste is much worse. Individualism and competition support and sustain inequality.[11] Cultural and economic environment impresses inequality, individualism and competition on the young minds and so children accept and practise these things as they grow up. Thus, our society is fragmented and deformed.

In our hierarchized society, the people in the lower rungs give away their power by feeling inferior while those in higher rungs unsurp their power by feeling superior to them. Some superior people feel guilty of their superiority and rescue the inferior people without being asked. The other superior people feel angry at the baseness of the interior people and persecute them. Thus, there are three roles—Rescuer, Persecutor and Victim which form a Drama Triangle according to Stephen Karpman. Everyone has a favourite role though people shift to other roles temporarily. Rescuing and persecuting make and keep people powerless and dependent. When parents rescue their children, they do the things that children can do for themselves. When they persecute children, they overcontrol and punish children for petty things. All this prevents children from growing fully and being independent.[12] This polarization of power causes political deformity.

Inequality does not confine to society but invades human body, mind and soul. Gender and social deformities are translated psychosomatically, leading to physical deformity. Intellectuals and women are generally weak and tender while workers are strong and tough. The organs having more exercise become stronger than those having less exercise. The strong adept right hand and the weak inept left hand are the product of this cultural programming. Since the body is considered base, its sensations are not allowed to reach the mind. This leads to the split and alienation between the body and the mind. This self-alienation kills spontaneity, spoils health and causes joylessness in addition to deformity. This often leads to drug addiction and abuse of sex.[13]

Human mind has two faculties: intuition and rationality. In men, rationality is encouraged more than intuition while in women, intuition is encouraged more than rationality. So in men, intuition remains repressed whereas in women, rationality remains repressed.[14] People become mad when their rationality is severely maimed. Lying is universal and children are trained intensely to lie and to accept lies so knowledge contains more falsehood than truth. Their rationality, intuition and feelings are often discounted. All this makes people mindless,[15] mentally deformed.

Culture and civilization desecrate human soul and break its primal unity. The forces of life and death become divided, differentiated, alienated and antagonistic.[16] The inner conflict and the scarcity of love caused by gender, social and political deformities distort and emaciate human soul. Lovelessness is encouraged as it facilitates exploitation, oppression and any gross atrocity. Real love is very rare and recognition, a poor substitute for love, is used for survival. People are love-starved and they are supplied recognition on ration as much as they are obedient to cultural norms. The people of higher rungs get much more recognition than those of lower rungs in the hierarchized society.[17] The inhuman crimes and atrocities are due to this spiritual deformity.

The studies of both science and theosophy reveal that these divisions and deformities are not inherent, neither biologically programmed nor divinely determined. They are culturally programmed and transmitted. This culture is man-made. But man "merely forgets that the world he lives in has been produced by himself."[18] So, he thinks that this culturally constructed world is real and eternal. He does not realize that "the reality of this world is not an intrinsic quality, nor is it given once and for all."[19] Hindu philosophy, therefore, considers this man-made world mythical, illusory. Culture is the network of illusions. Going beyond these divisions and deformities caused by culture and civilization, human beings have to seek salvation, *moksha*, through reunification, that is what religion etymologically means. Long aptly observes:

> Hindu literature and spirituality are informed by the condition that, as man and his world came into being through the disruption of a primal unity and as man is identified essentially (i.e., spiritually and ontologically) with that primordial reality, he will realize his highest ideal only by transcending this world of cosmic conflict and illusoriness and, thereby reintegrating himself with the source from which he and the cosmos emerged in the beginning.[20]

Human beings have to strip their souls of all the enveloping cultural layers and reach the inner core, their true nature, humanness on the one hand, and, on the other, they have to dissolve their cultural world in order to reintegrate with Nature. We have thus come to agree with Rousseau and say that since culture makes man morbid we have to go back to Nature. Until then, people will continue to suffer from various hydra-headed problems caused by our cultural deformity.

This is exquisitely exemplified in both the pre- and post-Independence Indian English drama. In the first, gender deformity is illustrated by Rabindranath Tagore and other dramatists. Tagore deals with the problems of women as a part of his plays. The eponymous character of *Malini* is a Buddhist princess. Fanatic Hindu Brahmins demand her banishment. Her unperturbed grace shocks them and changes their mind. In *Natir Puja* Srimati is a dancer in the court of King Ajatashatru. She offers her dance in her worship to God. She sheds all her adornments and emerges as a Buddhist nun with her yellow wrap during her dance. She is then killed at the command of the king. But these plays do not touch the suffering of women caused by patriarchy. However, the performance of *Natir Puja* raised many patriarchal objections and feminist questions about a woman's freedom as discussed by Rimli Bhattacharya in her paper.[21] In *Ama and Vinayaka*, Ama marries a Muslim. Her father kills the Muslim and her mother forces her to commit *Sati* on the funeral pyre of the Hindu bridegroom who is to marry her and who dies in a fight. *Karna and Kunti* shows Kunti's love for Karna whom she abandons as she is afraid of patriarchal values against pre-marital pregnancy.

Coming to the other minor dramatists of the pre-Independence period, Kailasam's *A Monologue* depicts how women depend on men. The play, thus, considers patriarchal culture to be real. Harindranath Chattopadhyaya's *The Parrot* shows how women, bound by cultural values, suffer intensely throughout their life. A.C. Krishnaswami exposes, in *The Two Twice-Borns*, the plight of young girls who are married to old men in olden days. V.V. Srinivasa Aiyangar, in *Blessed in a Wife*, shows how some men torture their wives by neglecting them and visiting concubines. V. Narayanan's *The Lawyer and His Daughter* deals with the suffering of the widows of higher caste Hindus. Balwant Gargi's *The Matriarch* condemns the suffocating authority of some mothers over their sons. Purushottam Tricumdas in *Sauce for the Goose* humorously portrays the rebellion of women against immoral men. The feminist leader, Sunitadevi challenges the patriarchal concept of chastity: "Chastity is not natural to women. It has been enforced by man to satisfy his vanity."[22]

Some of the plays during the second period, exemplifying gender deformity are as follows. *Alone in Ayodhya*, by Mathuram Boothalingam, presents women's problems and questions patriarchal practices. The theme is borrowed from the *Ramayana*. Sita argues with Rama and desires to participate in politics. Urmila, a woman of self-respect, takes Lakshmana to task for neglecting her and feeling too proud of his race. B.S. Kalsi's *The Little Dictator* portrays a patriarchal father. Mr. Pandit is dictatorial in his attitude towards his wife and children. He oppresses them and causes hatred, fear and disgust in them. Shiv K. Kumar's *The Last Wedding Anniversary* is about marital disharmony. Lalit, as sensitive as a woman, marries Rupa as ambitious and as sociable as a man. Their personalities are complementary so they become psychologically dependent on each other. Yet, their personalities remain alien to each other and loving relationship does not develop between them. The reappearance of Neela, Lalit's first love, precipitates their marital disharmony. Gender deformity is the source of the problems in these plays.

Again in the first period, passing on to social deformity, Rabindranath Tagore condemns the cultural oppression and economic exploitation of the people of lower castes and classes by those of the higher castes and classes. His *Chandalini* hints at how dalits are humiliated as untouchables. Anand, a Buddhist monk, drinks water poured by Prakriti, an untouchable girl. She sees for the first time a man who considers her human. This overwhelmingly pleases her and she falls in love with him at once. The aspect of renunciation in Buddhism renders her awakening futile. Since the Buddhist monk will not marry her, his treating her equally is of no use. In *Mukta-Dhara*, Tagore shows how science and technology are used in exploiting the people economically.

Kailasam goes to Indian myth to focus on the social deformity. Ekalavya in *The Purpose* and *Fulfilment* and Karna in *Karna*: *The Brahmin's Curse* are the greatest archers but they are not allowed to exercise their talent only because they belong to lower castes. The eponymous character of Keechaka lets himself be killed by Bhima, the husband of Draupadi, because he loves her honestly. R.G. Joshi points out: "Kailasam chose the characters from the *Mahabharata* and tried to interpret them in the light of human values."[23] Harindranath Chattopadhyaya exposes the exploitation of capitalism in *The Window* and that of imperialism in *The Sentry's Lantern*. V.V. Srinivasa Aiyangar shows, in *The Surgeon-General's Prescription*, how Sitapati tries to marry his daughter, Kamala to a rich old landlord against her wish and, in *The Point of View*, how the mother and the wife of Ramachandra Rao, a rich landlord, wait for his death to inherit his property. The plays illustrate how people become loveless in their mad scramble to the higher rung of the socio-economic ladder. Balwant Gargi's *The Vulture* depicts the inhuman exploitation of poor peasants by a landlord in a village. In V. Rampall's *Almighty Gold*, Krishenchander, an industrialist, worships gold and forces his son to marry a rich girl against his wish to marry a poor girl whom he loves. In Ranganath's *A Star is Born*, the corruption of doctors is exposed.

In the second period, social deformity is treated by a few playwrights. Asif Currimbhoy's *Darjeeling Tea* depicts the exploitation and oppression of the poor workers by the landlords of tea-estates. His *Inquilab* is about the Naxalite movement against the exploitation of poor peasants by landlords in villages. Radical students finally murder not only the landlord but also the Professor who is branded a revisionist.

Swami Avyaktananda in his collection of plays *India through the Ages* aims at dissolving social and religious distinctions through universal love. D.M. Borgaonkar in *Rakhi* ridicules the medieval concept of the superiority of blue blood. The Rana of Vijaygarh refuses to accept the donation of blood by the Rana of Vishalgarh for transfusion in the critical condition because the latter is inferior to the former. Later, the former accepts it when his wife ties a *rakhi* around the wrist of the latter. In his *The Temple Entry*, Mira, the daughter of the priest of the temple, leads Bijan and other untouchables into the temple against the inhuman tradition of untouchability.

As regards political deformity, in Indian English drama of the first period, Rabindranath Tagore in *The King and the Queen* shows how Queen Sumitra rescues King Vikram by looking after the administration while the king persecutes her by exploiting her kindness to indulge in sensual pleasures completely. Sumitra takes her brother's help from Kashmir to subdue the rebels. Vikram feels belittled by Sumitra so he wants to assert his power. He decides to make Sumitra humble and imprison Kumarsen, her brother. Sumitra still plays the Rescuer and finally sacrifices herself to gratify the ego of her husband. This deflates his ego and he feels powerless. The eponymous character of Sri Aurobindo's *Rodogune* loves Antiochus, a son of Cleopatra. Timocles, her other son, feels envious about it. Cleopatra favours Timocles because she cannot understand the honesty of Antiochus. Chancellor Phayllus and his sister exploit the rivalry between the brothers and make Timocles kill Antiochus. Rodogune also dies for her lover. Thus the power struggle makes people loveless and turns them against love.

Harindranath Chattopadhyaya in *The Window* illustrates how workers and poor people become powerless by accepting the social hierarchy and the theory of fate (*Karma*) that sustain exploitation. The worker thinks that the rich are fortunate because they buy God. His wife believes that it is their fate to be poor and to suffer. In V.V.S. Aiyangar's *Sub-Assistant Magistrate of Sultanpet*, Krishna Sarma gets promoted as the Sub-Assistant Magistrate of Sultanpet. He plays the Persecutor and abuses his power. Finally, he becomes the Victim when he is caught by the police.

In the second period, *The Dissident MLA* by Asif Currimbhoy which is based on the dissolution of the Gujarat Legislative Assembly in 1976 reflects contemporary Indian political scene. Manubhai is the fictitious MLA who becomes a dissident to have his own way. He instigates various agitations such as the *gherao* of the Vice-Chancellor by the students, a donkey-ride of a minister, loot, arson and many MLAs' breaking away from their party. All this leads to the dissolution of the Assembly and the imposing of President's rule. *Larins Sahib* by Gurcharan Das is about Henry Lawrence, a British Resident in Punjab. He is honest and faithful to the land. He loves Rani whom the British Government banishes against his wishes. Gradually he develops lust for power and assumes the authority of an 'Angrez-Badshah.' Finally he is dismissed from his post. In Manohar Malgonkar's *Line of Mars*, a royal family resorts to immoral means to sustain their power that they lose because of Dalhousie's cunning Doctrine of Lapse. In D.M. Borgaonkar's *Bhasmasura*, Professor Dinesh Chandra Buddhisagar, a scientist, invents a powerful destructive weapon, in his mad pursuit of power, through his intellect. He feels excited over the effectiveness of his invention which kills his wife. Thus, in our hierarchized society, people do not mind doing anything to reach the higher rungs of power.

Coming to physical deformity, in the first period, Rabindranath Tagore does not approve complete renunciation. He thinks that renunciation without love will not lead anybody to salvation and that bodily happiness need not be sacrificed. In fact, physical love alone takes one to the heights of spiritual love. His plays *Sanyasi* and *Chitra* illustrate this. In *Sanyasi*, the saint renounces all worldly pleasures and sits in meditation. Vasanti, a pretty lass, seeks his company but he runs away from her in panic. But he cannot run away from life. Finally, he realizes the truth and decides to embrace life. But the girl has already died. The eponymous character of Chitra loves Arjuna when he is an ascetic. she is granted celestial beauty for one year by the Gods of Love and Spring. Arjuna now cannot resist her charm and breaks his vow of celibacy. The physical beauty that has kindled love disappears. But their love does not confine to their body and it spreads to their mind and soul. Consequently, they overcome their temporary discontent and love each other honestly and passionately. By obeying one's body, one can overcome self-alienation and achieve the unification of one's body and soul.

Bharati Sarabhai, like Tagore, attempts to show in *Two Women* that salvation demands the unification of physical and spiritual fulfilment. Anuradha, an orthodox woman, marries Kanakaraya, an anglicised man. She believes in the religious ways of Hinduism and dislikes enjoying life while he wants to enjoy life. They decide to live their separate ways. At last, she realizes that the Himalayas, her religious refuge, can be found anywhere. Now she is ready to enjoy life with her husband but he dies of a secret disease. Urvashi, another woman in the play, is a widow and devotional singer who attempts to blend the physical and spiritual aspects of her life. In K.A. Abbas's *Invitation to Immortality*, the scientist invents the elixir that makes man immortal. He announces that he will give it to a person who convinces him of his worth. Various people like a film star, a British officer, a priest and a 'Hitler' try to convince the scientist of their worth but nobody succeeds. At last, a worker comes and tells them that *work is the real elixir of life*.

In the second period, *The Doldrummers* by Asif currimbhoy is about the poor young people who live on the pavements of such cities as Bombay. They are alienated and unhappy. They derive pleasure from drinking liquor, resorting to violence and committing fornication. In V.V. Srinivasa Aiyangar's *The Jolly Club*, the members enjoy drinking and gambling. They call their club South Indian Psychic and Spiritual Research Institute (SIPSRI). They feel elated not only in their self-indulgence but also in violating the prohibition secretly. The Police Commissioner is also a member of the club. He raids the club in order to please the minister. J.M. Lobo Prabhu's *Apes in the Parlour* is about the elite who seek happiness in illicit sex with Indira, a film star. Partap Sharma's plays *The Professor Has a Warcry* and *A Touch of Brightness* also deal with morbid sex.

In the first period, mental deformity finds a good illustration in Harindranath Chattopadhyaya's *The Saint* and *The Coffin*. There are more false saints than true ones. The saint, in the play, fools people by performing certain items of magic in the name of miracles. He leads corrupt life by exploiting the mindlessness of people. The play very successfully shows how religion is used to make and keep people mindless. *The Coffin* condemns the poets who tell lies to people through literature. Thus, they like saints, create false consciousness in people. The play also illustrates how parents and elders bring them up. Mohan, the central character, gets his daughter a cradle which looks like a coffin. The cradle, thus, symbolizes the burial of real consciousness. Mohan himself lives in the illusory world created by his aunt. At last, he comes out of it. Through him, the playwright conveys his message that the poet "should write about starving babies, about cruel masters, about poor sad women, about people who are shot because they asked for bread."[24]

The other plays of pre-Independence include V.V. Srinivasa Aiyangar's *The Two Selves*, Niranjan Pal's *The Goddess,* A.S.P. Ayyar's *In the Clutch of the Devil* and D.M. Borgaonkar's *Image-Breakers*. *The Two Selves* depicts the mental conflict of Sri Vasudeva Sarma. Saraswati Bai, his first wife does not bear him any children so he marries Dhani Bai. He starts loving his second wife more than the first one. He also begins drinking liquor. Gradually he experiences an inner conflict between his "Higher Self and Lower Self." *The Goddess* portrays how corrupt priests exploit people by using the name of religion. Abhiram, the chief priest at the temple of the Goddess, makes use of the blind faith of the people and amasses wealth. *In the Clutch of the Devil* also exposes the superstition of people and its exploitation by priests, astrologers, wizards and also money lenders. Raghavan and his wife believe that the death of their children is the result of black magic. So they spend a large amount of money on performing rituals to counter the black magic and punish the agent. But this benefits priests and money-lenders and drives Raghavan mad. *Image-Breakers* shows how religious faith maims human love. A number of yonger people form a league of Image-Breakers and rebel against the conventional marriage system.

In the second period, Asif Currimbhoy's psychological plays exemplify mental deformity. *The Clock* is about Henry, a neurotic. He resigns his job compulsively and rationalizes it. He then feels desperate and depressed. He is obsessed with love for his lady secretary. Later, his feelings of guilt take the form of two gunmen and his boss. He feels angry with his boss. Finally, he grows intolerant as he hears the clock tick and smashes it. But the noise does not stop. *The Dumb Dancer* portrays a Kathakali dancer who thinks that he is really Bhima, the character that he plays. Paradoxically, the psychiatrist, trying to cure him, becomes insane himself. *The Alien . . . Native Land* depicts the alienation of Jews in India and their psychological problems. *An Experiment with Truth* is about Gandhiji's life and his firm adherence to truth which is a real solution to mental deformity. In *Deep Roots* by Murli Das Melwani, Arvindo grows aware of the falsehood of customs, especially of marriage, and refuses to accept his father' choice. He exposes his friend's mercenary choice of a rich lame girl. Finally, he marries Neena ideally. Thus, he frees himself from the mental deformity of our morbid culture.

Spiritual Deformity is elucidated in the plays of Sri Aurobindo in pre-Independence period. All the five plays of Sri Aurobindo deal with love. In *Rodogune*, the eponymous character and her lover, Antiochus, fall victims to the power struggle. In *Perseus*, the eponymous character loves Andromeda and they together fight against Poseidon, the sea-god. In *Vasavadutta*, the eponymous character is a jailor but falls in love with Udayan, the prisoner and enemy of her father. In *The Viziers of Bassora*, Nureddene, the Vizier Alfazzal's son loves Anice, a slave-girl. Their love survives the plot of Almuene, the bad vizier. The eponymous character of *Eric* falls in love with Aslaug, the sister of his enemy. Similarly Aslaug who comes to kill Eric ends up in loving him. Thus love defeats hatred. Srinivasa lyengar observes: "All five plays underline the need for love, for Love alone is the great solvent of all varieties of evil. Love is supreme truth and goodness and power, and it can defy death and conquer it, and turn dross into gold."[25]

Tagore deals with the lovelessness of our culture in *Sacrifice* and that of civilization in *Mukta-Dhara*. Sacrifice is about the religious practice of sacrificing animals at the altar of Goddess Kali. The king is moved by the agony of Aparna, a beggar girl, whose goat is sacrificed so he forbids sacrifice. *Mukta-Dhara* shows how the products of science and technology are used to exploit and oppress people. The king constructs a dam to control the free flow of water. This makes his exploitation of Shivtarai for Uttarkut more effective than before. The Prince himself breaks it. Harindranath Chattopadhyaya's *The Sleeper Awakened* also criticizes loveless civilization.

CIVILISATION:	Then get out of the house.
SOUL FORCE:	That is not possible.
CIVILISATION:	I'll drive you out.
SOUL FORCE:	You cannot.[26]

The play conveys that love cannot be destroyed by civilization. In Bharati Sarabhai's *The Well of the People*, an old woman wants to go on a pilgrimage but realizes that service to mankind is service to God. She therefore spends her savings on building a well for the untouchables.

In thc sccond period, Asif Currimbhoy's plays *The Refugee* and *Sonal Bangla* depict the inhuman atrocities of the Bangla Desh war in 1971. Women were raped and their breasts were cut off. People were literally butchered. Among the soulless people, a few compassionate humane men can be found. For instance, in *The Refugee* Sen Gupta gives shelter to Prof Yassin, a refugee and Prof Mosin helps him get a job in the local university. D.M. Borgaonkar's *The Great Coward* and *The Refugee* deal with the miserable sufferings of the victims of the partition immediately after Independence. Lakhan Deb's *Murder at thc Prayer Meeting* exemplifies the spiritual deformity of the people who can assassinate Mahatma Gandhi who has always stood and striven for truth, non-violence and communal harmony. Like Sri Aurobindo, various playwrights through their plays have endeavoured to show how love cures spiritual deformity and its ill-effects. *India through the Ages*, a collection of plays on various religions of India by Swami Avyaktananda, preaches universal love and communal harmony and aims at dissolving social and religious distinctions. In *My Sons* of Mrs J.M. Billimora, five students of Bombay university give up their linguistic and religious differences and live together like brothers. Similarly, in *The Flute of Krishna* by P.A. Krishna Swami, Murali and Vidyaranya love each other though they belong to different castes; they think that they, like the flute, are the instruments of God to serve the humanity.

Thus, a brief survey of the pre- and post-Independence Indian

Drama in English reveals that it deals with a gamut of various problems of the individual and the society arising from gender, social, political, physical, mental and spiritual deformities. Although the focus, in each play discussed above, is on one cultural deformity, the other deformities are invariably touched upon. An attempt is made in the following chapters to treat the cultural deformity as reflected in the English versions of the select plays of Mohan Rakesh, a Hindi playwright (North), Badal Sircar, a Bengali playwright (East), Vijay Tendulkar, a Marathi playwright (West) and Girish Karnad, a Kannada playwright (South) who truly represent the modern Indian sensibility.

Mohan Rakesh is a famous Hindi short-story writer, novelist and playwright. He belongs to the modern Hindi literary movement of *nai kahani* (new short story). Some of his plays are first written as short stories. For example, *The Great Swans of the Waves* is first a short story. N. Choudhuri points out: "With Mohan Rakesh (1925-72) Hindi drama makes a departure from pseudo-modernism and traditional symbolism to the drama of 'non-communication'—the modern man's failure to understand himself or to understand the other person and their mutual failure to understand each other, which is the real tragedy of modern life."[27] Mohan Rakesh is greatly influenced by Marxism. He says: "We called ourselves progressive because most of us, including me, agree with the philosophical aspects of Marxist thinking."[28] Yet, he does not completely align himself with the die-hard progressives. Consequently, he is criticized by both progressive and non-progressive writers. He explains the difficult situation that he is in:

> that set of die-hard Progressives called us non-Progressive or anti-Progressives because we did not align ourselves with their way of thinking, which stated that writing is to be done according to slogans and manifestos. On the other hand, we also were condemned or rejected by those writers who were non-Progressives because, according to them, we were not neutral to the problems of our times, the immediate things around us . . . the writer should be above the immediate social situation. So it was a difficult situation in which we were all the time trying to establish our viewpoint.[29]

Like Dharamvir Bharati and Karnad, he also makes use of history and legend in *One Day in Ashadha* and *The Great Swans of the Waves* to throw light on contemporary problems. He justifies this: "I don't think that there's any harm in exploiting a particular character or situation in history for the sake of saying something modern, particularly if using such a character or situation would make it easier for the writer to do so."[30] His plays elucidate the suffering of men and women, especially at psychological level, as they fall victims to socio-economic hierarchy and cultural hegemony.

Girish Karnad is a great bureaucrat, famous TV and film artiste and director, and successful playwright. He wanted to become an English poet but he wrote his first play *Yayati* in Kannada. The play emerged from his resentment at being suffocated by the responsibilities his parents thrust on him. His other plays also show the strong impact of his rebellion against cultural hegemony. He borrows his themes from Indian history, myth and legend and employs in his plays the techniques of classical and folk theatre of India. On the one hand, he cannot waste his time on inventing new stories and on the other, he wants to make use of culture to destroy its own false values. So, he argues: "The energy of folk theatre comes from the fact that although it seems to uphold traditional values, it also has the means of questioning these values, of making them literally stand on their head."[31] He shares the disillusionment of modern Indian intelligentsia and he is not fascinated by Marxism as he realizes its limitations. He points out: "Even today Marxist ideologues are lost when confronted with native categories like caste."[32] Karnad borrows his themes from history in *Tughlaq* and *Tale-Danda*, from myth in *Hayavadana* and from folklore in *Naga-Mandala*.

Vijay Tendulkar is the avant-garde Marathi playwright and short-story writer. In the beginning, he was a journalist. Then he moved around and saw things closely. But he felt dissatisfied when he started writing editorials with information received from second-hand sources. He says: "It started with my journalistic dissatisfaction, but it grew into much bigger proportions, in the sense that it became a matter of conscience as a human being. I became restless."[33] He left journalism when he received Nehru Fellowship for the years 1973-75. During his travel throughout India, he saw directly all kinds of violence. From this experience, he infers: "Unlike the communists I don't think that violence can be eliminated in a classless society, or, for that matter, in any society. The spirit of aggression is something that the human being is born with. Not that it's bad. Without violence man would have turned into a vegetable."[34] Thus, he visualized both the positive and negative faces of violence. As a student, he worked in the 42 movement as a courier.[35] Regarding ideology, he says: "I do not align myself to any political ideology . . . I do have my sympathies with the left."[36] He was actively associated with the civil liberties movements. He exposes all kinds of inhuman violence in his plays. He never romanticizes his characters or situations. He is a prolific writer. Of his twenty-eight full-length plays, only seven have been translated into English.

Badal Sircar is a civil engineer and great Bengali playwright. Ella Dutta in the Introduction to *Three Plays* of Sircar writes: "Badal Sircar stands in the forefront of a new theatre movement in India. Both in form and content he has moved away radically from what the proscenium has to offer us today." (v) Sircar first wrote humorous plays during late fifties. Then, he wrote his plays of sombre existentialism during sixties. Finally, he evolved Third Theatre with the influence of Grotowski's Poor Theatre and Schechner's Environmental Theatre. Third Theatre is different from the urban proscenium theatre (the first theatre) and the rural folk theatre (the second theatre). It does away with all paraphernalia and is virtually free theatre. Sircar's focus shifts from the individual to the society in his existential plays of sixties and it is on the society in his plays of Third theatre. Sircar abandons plot and characterization in these latter plays because the sociological approach demands it. Sircar writes: "A character may be too limiting in its individuality, a story may be too specific to the subject."[37] He has sympathy for Communists yet he differs with them. Ella Dutta writes: "He does not wish to create new myths in place of the old. He prefers to raise the consciousness and create awareness of the issues." (viii) Sircar aims at effecting awareness in such a manner that it makes people feel guilty of their indifference. He does not attempt to give any clear specific solutions but only hints at them.

NOTES

1. Robert Wuthnow et.al., *Cultural Analysis* (Boston: Routledge, 1984) 23-24.
2. "Life out of Death," *The Hindustan Times*, 5 April 1992: 13.
3. Qtd. Kavita Nagpal, "The Badal Sircar Magic," *The Hindustan Times*, 5 April 1992: 13.
4. Mohan Maharishi, "Changing Role of Words in Theatre: Mohan Rakesh," *Sangeet Natak*, Oct.-Dec. 1971: 26.
5. Girish Karnad, *Hayavadana* (New Delhi: Oxford UP, 1988) 57.
6. Interpreted by Erich Fromm, "Marx's Contribution to the Knowledge of Man," *The Crisis of Psychoanalysis* (London: Jonathan Cape, 1971) 68.
7. Interview, *The Indian Express,* 27 March 1983, Magazine section, 5.
8. Frederick C. Gamst and Edward Norbeck, *Ideas of Culture: Sources and Uses* (New York: Holt, 1976) 152.
9. See Hogie Wyckoff, "Sex Role Scripting in Men and Women," *Scripts People Live,* Claude M. Steiner (New York: Bantam, 1980) 196-209.

10. See *Dr. Babasaheb Ambedkar: Writings and Speeches* (Bombay: Govt. of Maharashtra, 1987).
11. See Steiner, "Competition: The Banal Scripting of Inequality," *Scripts People Live*, 186-93.
12. See Steiner, "Rescue: The Banal Scripting of Powerlessness," *Scripts People Live*, 175-85.
13. See Steiner, "Basic Training: Training in Joylessness," *Scripts People Live*, 167-84.
14. See Wyckoff, "Sex Role Scripting in Men and Women."
15. Steiner, "Basic Training," *Scripts People Live*, 141-66.
16. See Norman O. Brown, *Life against Death* (London: Routledge, 1959).
17. See Steiner, "Basic Training," *Scripts People Live*, 125-40.
18. Wuthnow, 25.
19. Wuthnow, 15.
20. Long, 173.
21. Golay Memorial Seminar on Modern Dramatic Statement, University of Pune, Dec. 7-8, 1995. Unpublished.
22. (Baroda: n.p, 1944) 20.
23. *Myth in Indian Drama* (Delhi: B.R., n.d.) 128.
24. Harindranath Chattopadhyaya, *Five Plays* (Pondicherry, n.p, 1937) 138.
25. *Indian Writing in English* (New Delhi: Sterling, 1985) 231.
26. (Madras, n.d.) 88.
27. "Hindi Drama," *Comparative Indian Literature,* ed. K.M. George (Madras: MacMillan India, 1984) 512-13.
28. Interview, A *Journal of South Asian Literature,* Vol. IX, Nos. 2 & 3, 1973; 23.
29. *Loc. cit.* 23.
30. *Ibid.* 33.
31. Girish Karnad, "Author's Introduction," *Three Plays* (Delhi: Oxford UP, 1994) 14.
32. Karnad, 7.
33. Interview, *The Indian Express,* March 27, 1983 Magazine Section, 5.
34. Interview, *India Today,* Dec. 16-31, 1980, 157.
35. Priya Adarkar, "Vijay Tendulkar interviewed," *Enact*, Jan.-Feb. 1971:no page.
36. "No Ideology" (Interview), *India Today*, June 16-30, 1980; III.
37. Qtd. Gowri Ramnarayan, "The endless road of Badal Sircar's 'free theatre,'" *Frontline*, August 28, 1992, 75.

Gender Deformity: Tendulkar's *Kamala*, Karnad's *Naga-Mandala* and Rakesh's *Half-Way House*

SARITA: Listen to the story of how he bought the slave Kamala and made use of her. The other slave he got free—not just free—the slave's father shelled out the money—a big sum . . .

Kamala

In the beginning, this universe was nothing but the Self in the form of a man. . . . He was as large as a man and woman embracing. This Self then divided itself into parts; and with that, there were a master and a mistress.[1]

Quoted from *Brihadaranyaka Upanishad* by Campbell, this symbolizes the split of a whole human being into a man and a woman. The same symbolism can be found in the creation of Adam and Eve by God as described in the *Bible*.

We are born whole human beings, but gender-based division of labour breaks us into male and female fragments. Each fragment retains only half of the human potential. The retained part overgrows to compensate for the other part which remains underdeveloped. These two polarized, deformed fragments are called men and women. These gender deformities are thus caused and gradually 'canonized' by socio-cultural programming of sex roles. They are glorified and children are trained to attain them through socialization since their birth. Hogie Wyckoff, a Transactional Analyst, writes: "As women and men we are socialized to develop certain parts of our personalities while suppressing the development of other parts. This programming promotes a predetermined, stilted, and repetitive way of acting life."[2]

Every human being has the potential for nurturing, controlling, rationality, intuition, spontaneity and adaptation. To be masculine, men develop the faculties of controlling and rationality while suppressing those of nurturing and intuition. To be feminine, women develop the faculties of nurturing and intuition while suppressing those of controlling and rationality. To be cultured, both men and women develop the faculty of adaptation to culture (but not to Nature), while suppressing that of spontaneity and so neither enjoys life. Nurturing and intuition help women perform their culturally allotted function, child-rearing and house-keeping while controlling and rationality help men perform their culturally allotted function, bread-earning. Adaptation to culture and the lack of spontaneity make both of them obedient to their masters. Thus, men and women have become different, except in their obedience. These differences cause alienation and antagonism between men and women. So, they find each other mysterious and hostile.

Structure of Human Mind

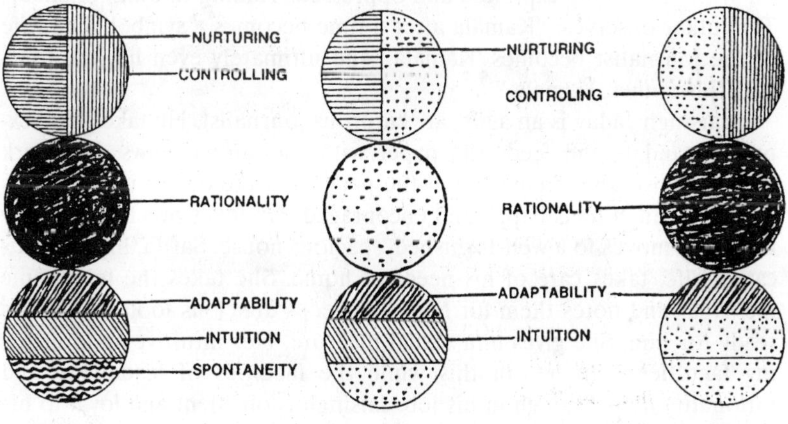

A Whole Human Being **A Feminine Woman** **A Masculine Man**

Gender deformity not only makes men and women incomplete human beings but enslaves them to the exploitative and oppressive society. Men are exploited and oppressed in the society while women are exploited and oppressed in the house. Men are content with their power in the house while women are content with their power over children and daughters-in-law. Like men, women are also divided and hierarchised class-wise and relation-wise. This causes alienation and antagonism between the women of the higher rungs (rich/higher castes/mothers-in-law) and those of the lower rungs (poor/lower castes/daughters-in-law). Men and women imbibe the exploitative and oppressive culture and perpetuate it. So, they never realize the reality. They blame one another for their miserable life and quarrel among themselves. But they are not united and do not collectively try to eradicate the morbid culture that brought about this pathetic state. That is why Claude M. Steiner talks about the liberation of men and women from sex role scripting.[3] Vijay Tendulkar and Girish Karnad are particularly provoked by gender deformity in Indian society.

Though all the plays of Tendulkar are concerned with gender deformity, his *Kamala* treats this cultural malady more elaborately. The play was inspired by a real life incident—*The Indian Express* expose by Ashwin Sarin, who actually bought a girl from a rural flesh market and presented at a press conference.[4] Jaisingh Jadav is a brilliant, brave journalist. He and Sarita, his sophisticated wife, remain ignorant of their being exploited and oppressed until Kamala, an uneducated tribal woman, triggers their awareness. In the play, Kamala becomes a powerful symbol of being exploited and oppressed. Talking to Sunil Shanbag, Tendulkar observes: "Kamala after a time becomes a symbol. The wife of the journalist becomes 'Kamala,' and ultimately even he [the journalist] becomes 'Kamala.'"[5]

Jaisingh Jadav is an agile, adventurous journalist. He takes risk, exposes scandals and feeds the paper with sensational news. His work greatly boosts the circulation of the paper and the owner increases his salary. Jaisingh feels happy and encouraged and takes much more risky tasks. He moves to a well-furnished, spacious house. Sarita, his sophisticated wife, takes care of his needs at home. She takes the telephonic messages and notes them for him. She keeps delicious food and drinks ready for him. She gives him sexual pleasure. Her intuitive and nurturing faculties help her in this while the faculties of leadership and rationality help Jaisingh in his job. Jaisingh is obedient and loyal to his master while Sarita is obedient and loyal to him. In such a sexist and familial system, a 'good' wife refreshes her husband so that he may work hard for his employer. So, it can be said as Steiner aptly points out: "In order for a man to be optimally exploited in his labour he must live with a woman who, on his eight hours of off-work time, re-supplies him with energy." (380-81)

Jaisingh goes to Luhardaga beyond Ranchi in Bihar and buys Kamala for Rs. 250 at flesh market where women of all kinds are auctioned openly. He brings her to Delhi and keeps her in his house to present her at a press conference in the evening in order to expose the inhuman trade. He keeps it secret even from his best friend, Jain, who just visits him in the forenoon. Individualism and competition of his profession demands it. Jain, knowing the hardships of Sarita, casually remarks: "Shame on you! Hero of anti-exploitation campaigns makes slave of wife"[6] and calls Sarita lovely bonded labourer while saying 'Bye.' This anticipates Sarita's sudden realization of her position in the family.

Kakasaheb, Sarita's uncle, who runs a paper, is there. He apprehends the predicament of Jaisingh. He forewarns him of the possible future danger: "You may be caught in a terrible jam some time." (9) This proves to be true later though Jaisingh ignores it. Kakasaheb later tries to convince him to leave such a job because it is not only dangerous but also inhuman. Jaisingh is not convinced as he is under the illusion that he is fighting through press against exploitation and oppression. He also credulously believes that his employer will protect him.

SARITA: Supposing you're sent to jail?

JAISINGH: I don't mind. My editor is going to fight this case right upto the Supreme Court. (26)

Jaisingh meticulously executes his plan and succeeds marvellously at the press conference in exposing the inhuman trade by presenting Kamala as a proof. Kamala is asked certain unpleasant questions there. But Jaisingh lacks the faculties of intuition and nurturing in this context and does not take notice of Kamala's embarrassment. Jaisingh and Jain are very much intoxicated by drinks and success while Kakasheb and Sarita feel very sorry for Kamala. So Sarita, being annoyed, refuses to sleep with him that night.

Sarita is disturbed and cannot sleep. Kamala comes and talks to her. She asks: "How much did he buy you for?" (34) This unexpected question enlightens Sarita on her position in the family. Though Jaisingh took a handsome dowry in marrying her, she feels like saying 'Seven hundred.' Kamala remarks, 'It was an expensive bargain, memsahib.' (34) She then proposes that she will do all the housework while Sarita will look after accounts and such 'sophisticated' things. She adds that each of them will share their master's bed half a month each. Sarita agrees to this. She realizes that she is also a slave like Kamala. The realisation is shocking and painful to her.

Jaisingh receives many compliments in the morning and feels very happy. As the police are after him to take custody of Kamala, he hastens to take her to the orphanage. Sarita opposes this and requests him to allow Kamala to stay with them in their house. Then, the dormant male chauvinist in him wakes up and says: "It's I who take decisions in this house, and no one else." (42) He takes Kamala to the orphanage and attends a party in the evening. What Simone de Beauvoir says about the modern men applies aptly to Jaisingh here: "The men of today show a certain duplicity of attitude which is painfully lacerating to women; they are willing on the whole to accept woman as a fellow being, an equal; but they require her to remain the inessential."[7] Sarita grows emotional and resentful at this. She proposes to hold a press conference to expose the tyranny of her husband. Kakasaheb tries to calm her by saying that it is common with men. He then confesses: "I gave your aunt a lot of trouble. As if it was my right. I didn't care what she felt at all . . . " (47) Then he adds that men are as humanly weak as women. But Sarita is not pacified.

Later, Jain comes and says that Jaisingh has been dismissed from his job by the proprietor under the pressure of very big people who are involved in the flesh market. Jaisingh, being called, returns home and learns about his dismissal. He loses his temper, curses his employer and decides to expose all his crimes at a press conference the following day. The nurturing faculty in Sarita overcomes her resentment and she tries to console her husband. But being exhausted, he collapses onto the sofa and falls asleep. Sarita does not give up her proposal but postpones it.

Sarita represents educated and sophisticated wives. They do not realise that their education makes them sophisticated slaves. As will be seen in mental deformity, education impoverishes our awareness. Jaisingh represents educated liberal middle-class men. They cherish the illusions of their freedom and liberalism. In crises, their hidden male chauvinism comes out. They do not know that they are exploited and oppressed by their employer as their wives are exploited and oppressed by them.

Arundhati Banerjee in 'Introduction' makes a concluding remark: "*Kamala* is an indictment of the success-oriented male-dominated society where women are often victims or stepping stones in men's achievements."[8] (xviii) But it can also be concluded that *Kamala* is an indictment of the business-oriented capital-dominated society where men like Jaisingh are victims or stepping stones in a capitalist's success.

Women are oppressed and exploited more than men in our society as it remains culturally patriarchal in spite of democracy. Women bear and bring up children; do all the house work and some of them do jobs additionally. Yet they are considered a debit to the family. They are ill-treated and tortured by their husbands and in-laws for various reasons. Ambedkar points out, "A woman under the laws of Manu is subject to corporal punishment and Manu allows the husband the right to beat his wife."[9] Indian society which has accepted the laws of Manu[10] denies women education and thus mental growth. Manu says, "Women have no right to study the Vedas."[11] In modern India, women are allowed to study so that they may become sophisticated slaves.

The plight of Hindu women is peculiar. Sudhir Kakar, a psychoanalyst, points out, "the mother—whore—partner-in-ritual trichotomy is crucial for understanding the culture's public and official attitude towards women and wives."[12] A Hindu wife is honoured as a mother to bear progeny for her husband and as a partner to him in performing religious rites. So Manu himself says, "Where women are honoured, there the gods are pleased."[13] But, she is feared and loathed as a whore. That is why Kakar observes:

> It is only as a 'woman' a female sexual being, that the patriarchal culture's horror and scorn are heaped upon hapless wife. It is clear from its context that the oft-quoted verse, 'Her father protects her in childhood, her husband protects her in youth and her sons protect her in old age; a woman is never fit for independence,' refers to a protection not from external danger but from the woman's inner, sexual proclivities . . . yet guarding her by force is not realistically possible and perhaps it is better if she is thoroughly engaged in household work and thus fancy free. (1)

She cannot thus even think of sex as she feels completely exhausted by the end of the day. Moreover as Jandhyala points out: "With woman's sexuality so closely bound with marriage and her role as wife and mother, there was no possibility of considering her sexual needs and desires."[14]

The essence of Hindu culture tacitly conveys, "No sex in marriage please, we're Indian" (1) as Kakar rightly puts it. So "This pleasure was to be sought by men from courtesans well versed in the arts, women by definition did not fit into the socially accepted norms of the respectable family women" as Jandhyala aptly points out. Therefore Appanna in *Naga-Mandala* visits his concubine though Rani, his wife, is very beautiful and Brahmins in *Ghasiram Kotwal* go to the courtesans.

Thus women are sexually oppressed. It is reflected in the concept of chastity, a patriarchal value. It is one of the most powerful yet invisible cultural fetters that have enslaved women for ages. There has been enough literature, both oral and written, glorifying this enslaving value and deifying the women characters who observed it faithfully. *The Ramayana* in which Sita undergoes the fire ordeal to prove her chastity to Rama has been the cultural guide to Indians for more than two thousand years. Extra-marital enjoyment for women is a taboo even in this ultra modern age. Jandhyala therefore observes, "For emerging middle class culture, women's sexuality was subsumed within her reproductive role. Any other expression which transgressed this norm was perceived as vile and wanton." That is why Miss Leela Benare in *Silence! The Court is in Session* is mercilessly attacked verbally in the name of mock-trial as she has committed fornication and Rani in *Naga-Mandala* is accused of adultery while the male culprits in both the plays are not found fault with. Condemning the sexual oppression of women by men, Jandhyala says, "It is desired that women have a choice, control over their bodies and lives." Benare says: "Who are these people to say what I can or can't do? My life is my own—I haven't sold it to anyone for a job! My will is my own. My wishes are my own. No one can kill those—no one! I'll do what I like with myself and my life!"[15] This is exemplified in Karnad's *Naga-Mandala* and Tendulkar's *Silence! The Court is in Session*.

Naga-Mandala is based on two Kannada folk-tales that Karnad heard from A.K. Ramanujan.[16] It was produced at the Guthrie Theatre in the U.S.A. and dedicated to Ramanujan who was overseeing its rehearsals before his death. Story, in the form of a beautiful young woman, narrates it to a playwright who is cursed with death for having bored his audience. She, like a Sutradhar or Bhagavata, conducts the play. Her presence adds to the feministic aura of the play.

Appanna marries Rani and brings her to his house when she reaches womanhood. She arranges for his bath and serves him lunch. After lunch, he locks her in and goes to his concubine. Rani feels lonely and miserable. Mentally she is still a child, craving for parental affection. So she moans 'Oh Mother! Father!' in her sleep. The following day, she expresses her fear of loneliness and Appanna discounts her feelings without any compassion:

APPANNA: What is there to be scared of? Just keep to yourself. No one will bother you. Rice! *(Pause)*

RANI: Please, you could —

APPANNA: Look, I don't like idle chatter. Don't question me. Do as you are told and you won't be punished. *(Finishes his meal, gets up.)* (7)

He locks her in and goes away as usual. She does housework mechanically. She daydreams that she is taken by an eagle to her parents who caress her affectionately. She sobs when she comes into the real world. She is confined to the kitchen. She is deprived of the affection of fellow-human beings and the knowledge of the outer world. She is practically imprisoned in a solitary confinement. Her personality therefore remains underdeveloped. She is thus made the weaker sex. Her being locked in symbolizes the chastity belt of the medieval ages. The empty house that she is locked in stands for her apathetic in-laws according to Karnad.[17]

Kurudavva, the friend of Appanna's mother, learns about Rani's suffering and gives her an aphrodisiac root. Rani follows her instruction and mixes the paste of the root in the curry to be served to her husband. Then, the curry explodes and boils over, giving away coils of pink steam. She is afraid that it may harm her husband so she throws it on the anthill. Appanna does not tolerate her going out for a moment and slaps her so hard that she collapses onto the floor. He, as a male chauvinist, expects his wife to serve him as a robot with absolute obedience.

Naga, a King Cobra, living in the anthill, consumes the curry and immediately falls in love with Rani. He assumes the form of Appanna and visits Rani at night. He commiserates with her over her pathetic condition and showers on her parental affection that she badly needs. All her pent-up sorrow bursts out. She feels relieved and happy. But she cannot comprehend the situation since Appanna cannot be so compassionate. Yet, she willingly suspends her disbelief and enjoys Naga's love and care. She feels happy and secure in his company. Appanna and Naga represent the two unconnected roles of a husband—'as a stranger during the day and as lover at night' according to Karnad.[18] Rajinder Paul rightly points out: "It is a play where a cobra plays the lover and proves to be better behaved than his human counterpart who is as insensitive as a husband as we read about in bad tales."[19] Rani falls asleep in his embrace and Naga feels happy about his success. He leaves before dawn.

Appanna comes in the morning the next day. Rani goes to him happily, only to find an expression of distaste on his face. She, therefore, thinks that she dreamt last night. Naga comes again that night and assures her that what she sees is real. Then, she asks him why he behaves differently at different times. Naga makes use of patriarachal authority to discount her reason and suppress her awareness lest his identity should be discovered:

NAGA:	*(Seriously)* I am afraid that is how it is going to be. Like *that* during the day. Like *this* at night. Don't ask me why.
RANI:	I won't. (23)

This injuction of Naga proves to be so powerful that Rani does not know his real identity until she sleeps with her own husband.

Rani enjoys Naga's affection and forgets herself in her happiness. Naga feels encouraged and makes love to her. When she realizes what Naga has done to her, she feels aghast. She at once moves away from him and weeps in a corner. She feels cheated into committing the horrible sin of sex. Naga is shocked at her erotic ignorance. He explains her how natural love-making is: "Frogs croaking in pelting rain, tortoises singing soundlessly in the dark, foxes, crabs, ants, rattlers, sharks, swallows—even the geese! The female begins to smell like the wet earth. And stung by her smell, the King Cobra starts searching for his Queen . . . everywhere, those who come together, cling, fall apart lazily! . . . It is there and there, everywhere." (25) But Rani is not convinced and says that they, unlike beasts, should have some sense of shame. Gradually, Naga's regular nocturnal visits cure her of frigidity and she starts enjoying erotic pleasure.

Rani becomes pregnant and feels elated that her nocturnal happiness is real. Naga is shocked to know this and afraid that his real identity will be detected. To the great confusion and chagrin of Rani, he asks her to keep it secret as long as possible. She can neither hide her pregnancy of five months nor have it aborted so she feels crest-fallen and helpless. The next day, Appanna discovers her pregnancy and is sure that she has committed adultery. This infuriates him and he kicks and curses her. She pleads her innocence as she knows that she slept with her husband only. But Appanna is not convinced as he never slept with her. He tries to smash her with a boulder but the Cobra saves her. He swears and goes out to request the village Elders to punish her.

Naga visits Rani that night as usual. He advises her to take the snake ordeal at the trial. When Rani innocently requests him to withdraw the case, he says that the trial is inevitable. He then assures her that everything will be alright: "All will be well. Don't worry. Your husband will become your slave tomorrow. You will get all you have ever wanted." (35) She suddenly runs to him and embraces him. She notices that his heart betrays his great anxiety. The mother in her tries to console him: "I mustn't let you go. I must listen to my heart and hold you back. Take you like a baby in my arms and keep you safe." (35) As she talks, Naga leaves quietly.

The village Elders sit in judgement the next day. They listen to Appanna and Rani. They ask Rani to prove her chastity by taking the oath while holding a red-hot iron rod. But she requests them to permit her to take the snake ordeal. As they concede to her request, she puts her hand in the anthill and takes out the Cobra. While holding it, she swears that she has never touched anybody other than her husband and the Cobra. The serpent spreads its hood over her head, sways it for a while and goes away. All the people prostrate before her, adore her as a Goddess and seek her blessings. Appanna also falls at her feet and begs for her forgiveness. Now he is her devoted husband and his concubine becomes her servant maid. Later Rani begets a beautiful boy. Thus she gets all as promised by Naga.

Naga-Mandala questions and exposes and gender-biased values and morals of patriarchy which have oppressed women for ages. This is effectively done by juxtaposing Appanna and Rani at the village court. Appanna enjoys extra-marital sex openly and unashamedly whereas Rani sleeps with Naga who assumes the form of Appanna. Everybody knows Appanna's relation with his concubine, yet the village Elders try Rani's case only. Thus, the play uncovers the injustice of the patriarchal moral code which demands the faithfulness of a woman to her husband but not the faithfulness of a man to his wife. Raju, therefore, points out: "His name means any Man and is a wry comment on any man who tries to enforce chastity on his wife while he himself indulges in extra-marital relationships"[20] Marulasiddappa expresses an opinion similar to that of Karnad: "The irony of the term 'fidelity' comes through in this sequence of events. Appanna and Naganna—two faces of one man, one seen at day, the other at night—symbolise the exploitation and double standards of man, while Rani is the symbol of a woman's eternal endurance of this oppression."[21]

Indian culture considers marriage to be the supreme boon of a woman because it offers her salvation through her service to her husband. For her, chastity is superior and preferable to life. This reduces her to a non-living commodity that her father offers as a gift (Kanyadan) to a man in marriage. She is denied love, enjoyment and education which are indispensable to the growth of her personality. Rani's situation is exactly this. So she is a simple, innocent and ignorant girl. She has grown physically but not matured mentally. She, therefore, behaves as a frightened child in Appanna's presence. Naga gives her love, enjoyment and some education too; so her personality grows. Consequently the little, helpless, diffident girl that she was gets transformed into a confident, courageous lady. She says: "I was a stupid, ignorant girl when you brought me here. But now I am a woman, a wife, and I am going to be a mother. I am not a parrot." (32) Appanna himself is shocked to see her boldness:

RANI: *(Snarling at Appanna)* If you don't let me go, I'll—*(Taken aback by her fury, Appanna lets her go.)* (38)

After the trial, Appanna accepts her superiority and obeys her.

The snake ordeal proves Rani's innocence and divinity to the world. Yet Appanna is not convinced as he knows that he has never slept with her. He says to himself: "Have I sinned so much that even Nature should laugh at me?" (41) As Rani sleeps with her own husband after the trial and as the bed manners of two men are always different, she discovers that Naga in the form of Appanna made love to her before the trial. Thus both Appanna and Rani know that she has lost her chastity. But they do not bother about it. Story aptly comments: "It is something one has to live with, like a husband who snores or a wife who is going bald." (41) The previous erotic experience perhaps makes Rani a better lover and Appanna enjoys marital bliss better than before. The loss of chastity therefore proves to be a kind of 'spell-break' to Appanna and Rani.

Vijay Tendulkar's *Silence! The Court is in Session* presents the same situation as that of *Naga-Mandala*. Leela Benare is a member of a drama troupe of amateur artists. In her teen age, she is seduced and sexually exploited by her own uncle. He does not marry her and her mother supports him. Benare overcomes the shock and completes her education. She becomes a teacher and earns good reputation as a teacher. Her academic interest takes her to Prof. Damle whom she respects for his scholarship and intelligence. Though married, he exploits her sexually and betrays her. She requests Balu Rodke and Ponkshe to marry her and save her from ignominy. But they are neither compassionate nor courageous to help her. Benare ridicules their diffidence. She is frank and open. She exposes the hypocrisy of people and laughs at their flaws. The other actors of the troupe are victims of her ridicule. So they plan to take it out on her. In the name of a mock-trial, they expose her private life, humiliate her and hurt her heart. They do not find fault with Prof. Damle, the real culprit who has spoilt her life. Concluding the trial, Sukhatme who is the counsel for prosecution in the mock-trial says to Kashikar, the judge:

> Milord, the nature of the charge against the accused, Miss Benare, is truly dreadful. The woman who is an accused has made a heinous blot on the sacred brow of motherhood—which is purer than heaven itself. For that any punishment, however great, that the law may give her, will be too mild by far. The character of the accused is appalling. It is bankrupt of morality. Not only that. Her

> conduct has blackened all social and moral values. The accused is public enemy number one. If such socially destructive tendencies are encouraged to flourish, this country and its culture will be totally destroyed. Therefore, I say the court must take a very stern, inexorable view of the prisoner's crime, without being trapped in any sentiment. . . . Woman bears the grave responsibility of building up the high values of society. '*Na stri swatantrya marhati*' 'No woman is fit for independence.' . . . That is the rule laid down for us by tradition. (114-15)

This is what our patriarchal culture makes us think. Like Appanna of *Naga-Mandala*, Prof. Damle is not punished for his sexual crime. Though men commit worst sexual crimes, people still say that women spoil the society. Men are tacitly permitted to seek extra-marital sexual pleasure while women's sexuality is limited to their motherhood within their marriage as Jandhyala points out. Leela Benare strongly protests against this inhuman oppression and demands freedom and right over her life to live her own way. She says: "Who are these people to say what I can or can't do? My *life is* my own—I haven't sold it to anyone for a job! My will is my own." (58)

Benare knows that jealous people are going to get her dismissed. Yet she is courageous. But the mock-trial has so severely hurt her that she breaks down completely. Utterly exhausted and agonised, she says: "*Na jeevan jeevanamarhati*. 'Life is not worthy of life.'" (116) Even Mrs. Kashikar joins the men in attacking her without any compassion. Like most of the women, she supports patriarchal values though they harm women. That is why the cynics of feminism declare that women are the enemies of women. But this is only because women are urged for their survival to absorb, observe and propagate patriarchal culture as aptly argued by Srilatha Batliwala in her brilliant article, "why do women oppress women?"[22]

Tendulkar's other plays also throw light on the plight of women in various situations. The eponymous character of *Sakharam Binder* keeps unlucky women who either left their husbands or who were left by them. Each woman has to do the housework and satisfy his sexual desire. He gives her food, clothing and shelter. Lakshmi is the seventh woman. Her husband leaves her because he thinks that she is sterile. As she cannot go anywhere, she accepts Sakharam. Sakharam criticises conventional husbands for their cruelty to their wives, but he himself proves worse than them. Lakshmi expresses this:

> I have never heard a kind word here. Always barking orders. Curses. Oaths. Threatening to throw me out. Kicks and blows. [*Wipes her eyes with the end of the sari.*] There I was in agony after I'd been belted, and all you wanted me to do was laugh. Laugh and laugh again. Here I am on the point of death and I'm supposed to laugh. Hell must be a better place than this.[23]

When Lakshmi cannot bear Sakharam's torture any longer, she leaves him for her nephew's house. Then, Sakharam brings Champa. Shinde, Champa's husband, tortures her sadistically by doing such awful things as putting chillypowder in her genitals. She leaves him as she grows courageous. She learns that Sakharam "really takes his money's worth out of a woman." (181) Yet she continues to live with him because "Instead of having ten beasts tearing at me every day, I'd rather do what one says to me." (184) Lakshmi accepts and observes patriarchal ethics while Champa rebels against them. When Lakshmi, driven by her nephew, returns to Sakharam, Champa protects her from Sakharam and allows her to stay with them. But Lakshmi betrays Champa who is therefore murdered by Sakharam.

In Tendulkar's *The Vultures*, Ramakant and Umakant plan to blackmail the lover of Manik, their own sister, for money. When they learn the lover is dead, they mercilessly kick Manik on the abdomen and cause abortion. In his *Ghasiram Kotwal*, the eponymous character offers his own innocent daughter to Nana to satisfy his lust and thus buys power from him to avenge his humiliation on the people of Poona. In his *Kanyadan*, a Gandhian ideally gives his daughter in marriage to a dalit boy. The dalit husband ill-treats his Brahmin wife who therefore returns to her father. The play shows that the position of women in India is worse than that of the dalits who have been oppressed, humiliated and exploited by caste Hindus for ages. Tendulkar's plays expose the oppression, exploitation and humiliation of women by their father, brother, husband, friend, colleague, officer and finally the other oppressed people who can be dalits or fellow-women.

Mohan Rakesh depicts gender deformity in *Half-Way House*. It is about the half and incomplete life of a middle-class family. Mahendranath is very convivial and his friends like his company. He marries Savitri. He enters into business with his friend, Juneja while she does a job. She urges him to get good furniture and other things for their house. He, therefore, withdraws his capital part by part, buys all the items one after another and furnishes the house according to the taste of his wife. Consequently he loses his business and feels bad about it. His wife goes on nagging him for losing business. This adds to his frustration and he takes it on his wife. As he does not fit her concept of a masculine man, she considers him impotent. She blames his parents first and his friends later for this. She runs after several men but fails to establish a relation with anyone of them. She feels greatly frustrated and takes it on her children. All this makes their house a vertiable hell.

The play starts with a prologue by the Man in a Black Suit. It conveys that all men behave alike in a given situation, a middle-class family here. The play proves this through Savitri, the central character. As Act I begins, she is seen tidying the living room. Mahendranath neither does any job nor helps his wife in housework. She says: "Idle all day but he can't look after his clothes . . . or even clear the table! Everything's left for me to do."[24] Then the First Man (her husband) comes. She takes him to task for not helping her in housework. She then refers to his being lazy. He admits that he has lost business as he spent his capital. She requests him to stay and meet her boss but he refuses to do so. Meanwhile their older girl, Bina, comes, leaving her husband. She and her husband cannot live in harmony because she carries with her the sexist culture from her parents and because it causes alienation between men and women. Bina says to her parents: "That the longer two people live together . . . the more estranged they become from one another." (4) She cannot understand why this happens. After the First Man leaves, the Second Man (Savitri's boss) comes. He looks important and speaks some nonsense. Savitri requests him to get her son a job. After her boss goes away, she asks her son not to ridicule her boss and to respect him. She feels annoyed as he does not show any interest. So she says to her children: "Very well, then. From now on I'll only bother about myself . . . you look after your own lives." (9)

In Act II, the older girl and the boy discuss the issues about their family. The boy tells her that Juneja, their father's friend, wants to speak to their mother. Their father has not come home and their mother has been in a bad mood. The boy feels that it is 'high time the situation changed.' The older girl feels like a stranger. Both of them think that there is something in their house that causes all this. Then the younger girl comes, quarrels with the boy and leaves. Their mother comes and says that Jagmohan is taking her away. She is informed that Juneja wants to talk to her. She does not like it. She says to the older girl, "When you come next time I may not be here." (11) She goes out with Jagmohan when he comes. As he cannot accept her so late in life, she feels utterly frustrated and comes home. She therefore treats the younger girl more harshly than her mischivous behaviour really deserves. Juneja comes and talks to her. He explains how her concept of a real man has marred her marital life. He points out:

> The point is that if any of these men had been a part of your life instead of Mahendra, you'd still have felt that you'd married the wrong man. you'd still have encountered a Mahendra, a Juneja, a Shivjeet or a Jagmohan and thought and reacted in the same way. Because the meaning of life to you is how many different things you can have and enjoy at the same time. One man alone could never have given them to you, so no matter who you married, you would always have felt as empty and as restless as today. (16)

Thus she wants a masculine man who can provide her all material luxuries. This involves sexist culture on the other. But the woman does not accept it and still says about her husband contemptnously: "I've absolutely no need for this 'pawn' as you say, this man who neither moves ahead himself nor permits anyone else to do so!" (17) To follow her idea, Mahendranath has to exploit others or let himself be exploited by others. Thus the play shows how not only men but also women perpetuate gender deformity.

Sircar's miniplay, *Marital* also presents the banal and disharmonious marital life of middle-class couples. Sircar is interested in the social dimension of the problems rather than the individual one. In his *Stale News*, the exploitation of women is hinted at. THREE says, "Offices are closed on Sundays, half days on Saturdays. But there's no holiday for me. I had to light up the oven at daybreak, and I've been on my feet ever since."[25]

The discussion shows that both men and women suffer on account of gender deformity. Tendulkar's *Kamala* illustrates how women are exploited at home while men are exploited at work. Karnad's *Naga-Mandala* and Tendulkar's *Silence! The Court is in Session* challenge the gender biased justice which favours men. Tendulkar conveys in his plays that women are oppressed by men irrespective of their relation to them—a wife in *Kamala*, a sister in *Vultures*, a daughter in *Ghasiram Kotwal*, a concubine in *Sakharam Binder* and a colleague in *Silence! The Court is in Session* are exploited and oppressed. Tendulkar's *Kamala* and Rakesh's *Half-Way House* depict how men are also the victims of our sexist culture. This proves that not only women but also men are made by our culture. The alienation and the consequent break-down of communication between men and women are portrayed in *Half-Way House*. The violence of men on women in Tendulkar's plays brings out the fact that men become inhuman in order to be masculine. Thus gender deformity is very comprehensively exemplified in Tendulkar's plays.

NOTES

1. Joseph Campbell, *The Masks of God: Oriental Mythology*, (Harmondsworth: Penguin, 1976) Vol. II, 9-10.
2. "Sex Role Scripting in Men and Women," *Scripts People Live*, Claude M. Steiner (New York: Bantam, 1980) 196.
3. Claude M. Steiner, *Scripts People Live*, 371-83.
4. Arundhati Banerjee, Introduction, *Five Plays* by Vijay Tendulkar (Bombay: Oxford UP, 1992) xvi.
5. 'I am against sensational journalism,' *The Sunday Observer*, October 1982.
6. Vijay Tendulkar, *Kamala*, *Five Plays*, trans. Priya Adarkar, 17.
7. *The Second Sex*, trans. H.M. Parshley (New York: Penguin, 1972) 291.
8. The victims or stepping stones in Jaisingh's achievement are Sarita, his wife, Kamala bai, their servant-maid and Kamala, the tribal woman that he bought.
9. *Dr. Babasaheb Ambedkar: Writings and Speeches* (Bombay: Education Dept., Govt of Maharashtra, 1987) Vol. 3, 431.
10. Manu is an ancient Hindu Lawgiver and his laws are widely accepted and observed.
11. Qtd. Ambedkar, 431.
12. Sudhir Kakar, "Marriage: War between the Sexes," *The Indian Express* Sunday Magazine, 7 June 1987, 1.
13. Qtd. Sudhir Kakar, 1.
14. Jandhyala Kameswari, "At his majesty's pleasure," *The Indian Express*, Weekend Magazine, 25 Nov. 1989, III.
15. Vijay Tendulkar, *Silence! The Court is in Session, Five Plays*, 58.
16. Girish Karnad, Preface *Naga-Mandala* (Delhi: Oxford UP, 1990).
17. "Author's Introduction," *Three Plays* (Delhi: Oxford UP, 1994) 17.
18. *Loc. cit.*
19. "Karnad Plays with a Cobra," *The Book Review*, July-Aug. 1990, 31.
20. Anand Kumar Raju, "A theatrical tour de force," *The Hindu*, Sunday Magazine, 29 Nov. 1992, IV.
21. "Drama's turning point," trans. Chaitanya, *Spectrum*, 11 June 1994, IV.
22. "Why do women oppose women?" *The Hindu,* Sunday Magazine, 2 May 1993, III.
23. Vijay Tendulkar, *Sakharam Binder,* trans. Kumud Mehta & Shanta Gokhale, *Five Plays*, 148.
24. Mohan Rakesh, *Half-Way House*, trans. Bindu Batra, *Enact*, May 1971.
25. Badal Sircar, *Stale News,* trans. Samik Bandyopadhyay, *Three Plays* (Calcutta: Seagull, 1985) 100.

Social Deformity: Karnad's *Tale-Danda*, Sircar's *Stale News* and Rakesh's *One Day in Ashadha*

> From this moment all *sharanas*, foreigners, and free thinkers are expelled from this land on pain of death. Women and the lower orders shall live within the norms prescribed by our ancient tradition, or else they'll suffer like dogs.
>
> *Tale-Danda*

> Disregarding for the moment the ideological distinctions among various Vedic cosmogonies, they all seem to be in agreement concerning one matter: the world we live in and know it emerged from a powerfully disruptive partition of a precosmogonic unity in accordance with the dictates of the law of necessity (Rta).[1]

The Vedic cosmogonies thus symbolically reveal that the division of labour is an indispensable evil of civilization. These divisions did not remain horizontal for long but were hierarchized by the human urge to overcome the feelings of inferiority caused by the alienation of human beings from Nature and to prove their power and superiority. The hierarchization, a major process of civilization, gave rise to competition which replaced cooperation. And the urge for superiority, as Adler would have argued, effected privatization, another major process of civilization. This process caused private family and private property. Even human love underwent privatization and so individualism emerged and replaced collectivism. Hierarchization and privatization have supported and sustained each other. All this has caused and consolidated social deformity and inequality.

Exploitation and oppression have become a 'natural' norm in our society as it has absorbed and observed individualism and competition. Consequently everybody takes inequality for granted. Steiner aptly points out, "The difficulty which we have in feeling equality with all other human beings is the result in part of our banal training in competitiveness and individualism."[2] He later talks about the dehumanizing effect of competition: "In our mad scramble to the top we forget how to love, how to think, and we lose track of who we are and what we really want." (187) Marx also comments on the evil effects of the division of labour and social deformity: "It proved, incontrovertibly, the disastrous effects of machinery and division of labour; the concentration of capital and land in a few hands; over-production and crises."[3]

The social deformity in the Hindu society took the form of 'caste system.' The Hindu society consists of four recognized classes called *Varnas* and one unrecognized class called *avarnas*. They are Brahmins (priests, poets, teachers and ministers), Kshatriyas (Kings and Warriors), Vaishyas (tradesmen), Shudras (craftsmen) and Panchamas (menial workers). Shudras and Panchamas toil and produce wealth which the people of higher classes enjoy. According to a Hindu myth, the four recognized classes emanated from the mouth, the arms, the thighs and the feet of Brahma, the God of Creation, respectively. Such myths and literature, created and perpetuated by Brahmins, seek to justify the social hierarchy and sanction their superiority. Stanley Rice rightly observes:

> If, then, it be admitted that Brahmans, at least in the earlier stages, became the superior caste by reason of their priestly office and all that is thereby implied, it is not unnatural that they should have made use of their position to glorify themselves, as the priesthood has shown itself apt to do in other countries. That they did this in extravagant fashion, claiming privileges unheard elsewhere and even arrogating to themselves the position divinities[4] may be admitted.[5]

Shudras and Panchamas are subdivided into various castes. Ambedkar elaborates on this: "Caste system is not merely a division of labourers—which is quite different from division of labour—it is an hierarchy in which the divisions of labourers are graded one about the other."[6] The gradation of the various castes of labourers prevents them from being united and makes them easily exploitable. Moreover Manu says: "A Brahmana may compel a Shudra, whether bought or unbought, to do servile work; for he is created by the Creator to be the slave of a Brahmana."[7] He prescribes severe punishment to Shudras for reading Vedas[8] and for insulting higher caste people. Panchamas are humiliated, oppressed and exploited more than Shudras for they are considered untouchable. This is the most inhuman part of Hindu culture and so Gandhiji considers it a great stigma on Hinduism. Since caste system gives Brahmins and other higher castes a privileged position, they have never tolerated any violation, including an inter-caste marriage and have punished the people most cruelly for violating the conventions of the caste system.

The social deformity of the Hindu society has not changed much for ages. Gross atrocities are committed on Shudras and Panchamas by high caste Hindus at one place or another, even now in the modern age of democracy.[9] Like Mulk Raj Anand and Bhabani Bhattacharya in Indian English fiction, Girish Karnad, Badal Sircar and Mohan Rakesh in Indian English drama are concerned with social deformity and expose the evil effects of caste and class in their plays, particularly in *Tale-Danda*, *Stale News* and *One Day in Ashadha*, respectively.

Karnad's *Tale-Danda* exposes the ugly deformity of the Hindu society by depicting the twelfth century communal struggle in the city of Kalyan in North Kanara when Bijjala was the king. In his court, there were great scholars and poets. Basavanna, the king's officer and the great poet-philosopher, united those brilliant people and fought for equality. They shed their castes and became *sharanas* or devotees of Lord Shiva. They talked about God in the language of common people. They considered their body the very abode of God and denounced idolatry. They condemned all the inhuman traditions and believed in social and gender equality. Finally their noble movement ended in a disaster when the marriage of a Brahmin girl to a Panchama boy led to the fateful war between *sharanas* and orthodox people.

Bijjala, a Shudra, a barber by caste, becomes the king of Kalyan. He himself says how he has become a Kshatriya: "For ten generations my forefathers ravaged the land as robber barons. For another five they ruled as the trusted feudatories of the Emperor himself. They married into every royal family in sight. Bribed generations of Brahmins with millions of cows. All this so they could have the caste of Kshatriya branded on their foreheads."[10] Bijjala also marries a royal princess, Rambhavati and has a son, Sovideva. He loves Sovideva but detests his unprincely behaviour. So he does not favour him while he makes the sons of his other wives local lords. Sovideva resents this greatly.

Bijjala knows that the people of higher castes do not respect him properly. He admits: "In all my sixty two years, the only people who have looked me in the eye without a reference to my lowly birth lurking deep in their eyes are the *sharanas*: Basavanna and his men." (15) Moreover his city flourishes because of their hard work and devotion. While accounting for his love of *sharanas*, the king himself says:

> Every *sharana* seeks only to earn the day's keep, makes no extra demands, treats profits with contempt. So who profits? From

every corner of the country, trade and commerce have come pouring into Kalyan, and now the city is bursting at its seams with money and activity. Even those who despise the *sharanas* for their beliefs need them for their economic enterprise—as indeed I do—and they pour money into the *sharana* coffers. .(24)

Thus Bijjala feels grateful to Basavanna and his men. But his son, Sovideva is not happy about it. He dislikes Basavanna and his philosophy. He knows that Basavanna spends large amounts of money on his hospitality to his guests. So he suspects that Basavanna has stolen money from the royal treasury. He therefore decides to prove this by opening the treasury. Thus, he wants to win his father's favour by making Basavanna unpopular.

Jagadeva, a *sharana*, comes to know Sovideva's plan to open the royal treasury. At once, he gathers thousands of *sharanas* and encircles it. Thus, he prevents Sovideva from tampering with it. Meanwhile Basavanna comes and immediately sends Jagadeva to attend his ailing father. He takes Sovideva into custody, finds the treasury intact after verification and then releases him. People consider it miraculous that the treasury is intact. Bijjala scolds Sovideva severely for his misdeed. So, Sovideva feels deeply frustrated, humiliated and hurt. He, therefore, decides to avenge this on his father and Basavanna. Damodara Bhatta, Queen's priest and Manchanna Kramita, the Brahmin adviser to the king, are very unhappy about Basavanna's mission and Bijjala's support to it. So, they join hands with Sovideva in the plot against Bijjala and Basavanna.

Jagadeva goes home and finds his father on death bed. His father's death makes him remorseful of neglecting home and so performs all the funeral rites for his father though it is contrary to his new faith. His emotion gets reversed as Basavanna visits him to express his condolences. Disturbed by the feelings of guilt for betraying the *sharana*-faith, Jagadeva blames Basavanna for his bereavement. He complains that Basavanna gets the credit though he prevented Sovideva from tampering with the treasury. Basavanna repudiates the miracle attributed to him and criticizes miracle-mongers for this. He is on his way to Maddur to stop the violence of *sharanas* against Jains which Jagadeva approves. He, then, condemns all violence whatever may be its cause. He understands the agitated soul of Jagadeva and pacifies it through prayer. Then he goes out to see the people who are clamorous for his *darshan*.

Sharanas assemble at Basavanna's house. They propose the marriage between Kalavati, a Brahmin girl and Sheelavanta, a *dalit* boy. Their parents invite Basavanna to the betrothal. Basavanna is shocked so much that he cannot say anything. *Sharanas* are unhappy about his hesitation. So Basavanna explains his apprehension: "It's a question of life and death for these children. From tomorrow the wrath of the bigoted will pursue them like a swarm of snakes, to strike as they pause to put up a roof or light an oven. Who will protect them then?" (38) Overwhelmed by the fervour of performing an inter-caste marriage, *sharanas* misunderstand Basavanna.

Basavanna, then, asks Sheelavanta for his opinion about the marriage. Sheelavanta likes Kalavati but does not want to marry her because she cannot stand even the smell of leather. Then, Lalita, the bride's mother, confirms his statement. Haralayya, the bridegroom's father, regrets that his son will not be allowed to change his vocation by other castes on account of the rigidity of the caste system. Lalita aptly quotes the intuitive prediction of Haralayya's mother: "Rivers of blood will flow if the marriage takes place." (41) Madhuvarasa, Lalita's husband, feels angry with her and orders her to keep quiet. Immediately, Gangambika, Basavanna's wife strongly objects to his male chauvinism: "Women and cattle, they are all the same to you, aren't they?" (42) In spite of all the discussion, *sharanas* stubbornly stick to their stand and one of them questions Basavanna: "So how many more generations have to roll by before a cobbler marries a Brahmin?" (44) At last Basavanna gives blessings and *sharanas* leave.

Bijjala requests Basavanna to stop the inter-caste marriage as it leads to communal violence. Basavanna replies that he cannot make decisions for *sharanas*. He will sit with his *sharanas* in front of his palace if Bijjala bans the marriage. Bijjala knows that the act of Basavanna will paralyse the life of Kalyan. So, he uses his army to avert the blood-bath during the marriage. Thus, the marriage takes place peacefully. While *sharanas* feel jubilant about their great achievement, the marriage infuriates orthodox Hindus.

Damodara Bhatta rushes to Indrani's house in the Courtesan's Quarter to talk to Sovideva about the marriage. Indrani, the courtesan, sees no reason in their going hysterical about it. So, Damodara explains her how the inter-caste marriage is a great sacrilege: "Indrani, the Rig Veda tells us that the four Varnas flowed out of the Primordial Man: the Brahmin from the head, the Shudra from the feet. So what we have here in this wedding is desecration of the body of the Purusha. How horrifying!" (55) Indrani is not convinced and praises Basavanna and his followers: "But the *sharanas* have done so much for the downtrodden and the destitute." (56) Damodara criticises Bijjala for protecting the *sharanas*. As Manchanna arrives with some courtiers, tradesmen, soldiers and citizens, he starts proclaiming the titles of Sovideva as if he had become the king of Kalyan.

Sovideva, Damodara and Manchanna hatch a plot against the king. They first get the loyal servants of Bijjala killed and then imprison him in his own palace. Basavanna knows this and requests *sharanas* to stand by the king. But most of them refuse to save him from Sovideva. So he himself, followed by a few *sharanas*, visits Bijjala who is greatly perturbed. He advises him to cling to Lord Shiva who alone can save him from any danger. As he leaves for Kappadi, Bijjala frenzily sobs and laughs.

Sovideva follows the advice of Damodara and Manchanna and persecutes the *sharanas* violently and mercilessly. As Basavanna is away, the *sharanas* lose heart and go helter-skelter. Damodara and Manchanna feel satisfied with it. But Manchanna is afraid of Basavanna: "The *sharanas* have lost their drive and in course of time are bound to revert to caste for sheer survival. Unfortunately Basavanna is alive and we can take nothing for granted." (79) Damodara pleads with Sovideva for forgiveness and generosity. But Manchanna advises him to get all the *sharanas* decimated without any discrimination and pay a brief visit to his father-in-law for his safety. Sovideva therefore leaves with Damodara, keeping Manchanna in charge of the kingdom.

Jagadeva and other *sharanas* are enraged about the persecution of their fellow-*sharanas* by Sovideva. So, they decide to avenge this on Sovideva. For this, they enter the palace through a secret passage. But, they do not find the Prince and feel greatly frustrated. Jagadeva leads them to the inner shrine of Shiva where the old king hides. Bijjala firmly embraces the *Linga*[11] to protect himself. Then, Jagadeva lies that Basavanna has sent them to him. Believing this, Bijjala comes out of the shrine. In spite of the request of the other *sharanas* not to kill him, Jagadeva stabs him to death. When they all leave on his request, he commits suicide. Basavanna returns from Kappadi and learns all this. He is greatly agitated and talks to himself philosophically.

Sovideva learns from messengers that 'the city reels under gruesome tales of rape, murder, looting and rioting.' (89) He blames Damodara for this. He orders the guard to shut him up when Damodara tries to reply. The guard kills him at once. Another messenger says, "The *sharanas* flee Kalyan." Sovideva then instructs:

> Pursue them. Don't let them escape. Men, women, children—cut them all down. . . . From this moment all *sharanas*, foreigners, and free thinkers are expelled from this land on pain of death. Women and the lower orders shall live within the norms prescribed by our ancient tradition, or else they'll suffer like dogs. Each citizen shall

> consider himself a soldier ready to lay down his life for the King. For the King is God incarnate! (90)

The crowning ceremony of Sovideva goes on as the city of Kalyan is ablaze. The screams of the victims and the eulogies of Sovideva by Brahmins are heard simultaneously.

Karnad says: "you can perceive deep irony, because, after all the martyrdom of the *sharanas*, when they re-emerged after three centuries of underground survival as lingayats, they were totally caste-ridden."[12] It happened as Manchanna had predicted, "The *sharanas* have lost their drive and in course of time are bound to revert to caste for sheer survival." (79) Karnad tries to trace the cause behind the failure of Basavanna's movement, "Ultimately the final betrayal was not by the enemies, but by the followers." He feels that *Tale-Danda* is relevant even today as religious fundamentalism is strong enough to destroy the Babri masjid and claim the lives of thousands of people. He adds: "When people all around us are slaughtered in the name of a temple, I hear echoes from those times long past."[13] That is why the words of Basavanna point to mandir-masjid violence: "Violence is wrong, whatever the provocation. To resort to it because someone else started it first is even worse. And to do so in the name of a structure of brick and mortar is a monument to stupidity." (29) Therefore what happened in the twelfth century is still happening now. So Karnad rightly remarks: "It seems 800 years have solved no problems. We are back exactly where we started."[14]

Badal Sircar also conveys through his play, *Stale News*, that the social inequality, oppression and exploitation have not changed even a little till today. For this, he narrates the Santhal Revolt that took place more than a century ago when the British were ruling India. And he juxtaposes the gross atrocities of oppression and exploitation of colonial India and those of post-colonial India. The statement that Man is the greatest creature on Earth is repeated several times as a refrain along the narration of instances of oppression and exploitation in the play. The irony is deep and deflates the human arrogance by stripping the social deformity of its ornaments and garments of civilization.

Stale News is the result of the collective work of Sircar and other members of Satabdi team. They have collected various news items of the exploitation and oppression and made a collage that portrays man. The play has got neither characters nor a story because 'A character may be too limiting in its individuality, a story may be too specific to suit his subject'[15] as Sircar puts it. K. Venkateswarlu rightly observes that what the Dead Man observes is the play and compares him to Tiresias of *The*

Waste Land by T.S. Eliot.[16] The Dead Man symbolises the dead humanity. He shows his left palm for the past and his right palm for the present. ONE is a middle-class urban young man who is exposed to various statements, news items and historical accounts narrated, reported and mimed by others. The play is acted by a chorus of eight people without any particular name.

ONE says, 'Man is the greatest creature on Earth' as the play begins. The actors mime the birth of ONE and then they attend to his education from school to college:

TWO.	Tuesday! Thursday! Sunday!
THREE.	Venus! Moon! Rahu! Ketu! . . .
SIX.	S is equal to vt plus ut square.
SEVEN.	The basic elements of production are land, labour, capital and organization
EIGHT.	Indian administration is structured within the framework of parliamentary democracy.[17]

As ONE grows, he is bombarded with various news items and statements and he also learns about the Santhals and their revolt. He also observes life around him. He is too confused to take any decision. But he continues his routine life. He completes his studies, gets a job and marries a woman.

The Santhals and similar ethnic groups came to India and settled in Bihar in pre-historic times. According to scholars, they were the first in India to cut down the forests, to set up homes and to discover agriculture eventually. When the state of Bihar came under the British rule, their barter-based economy and social life began to crumble under the impact of the exploitation and oppression of the British merchants and the money-based economy that those merchants introduced. The Santhals began to emerge into the open from the almost complete insularity that they had enjoyed in their social life for thousands of years. They started to spread over various areas in Bihar and Bengal around the year, 1790. The part of Bhagalpur where the Santhals formed a majority of population was known as Damin-i-ko or the Santhal Pargana. Bands of money lenders—Bengalis, Punjabis, Bhojpuris, Bhatias—converged on Damin-i-ko. They were called Dikus by the Santhals. They lent them small sums of cash, tobacco or cloth and bought their produce far below the reasonable price. The rates of interest were exorbitant, going up to five hundred percent at times. The Santhals had to sign a bond of perpetual slavery to get loans. As long as the loan was not repaid, the Santhal and his wife and children had to be the slaves of the moneylender. Thanks to an exorbitant compound interest and tampering with accounts, the loans never got repaid and the slavery became hereditary. If one such slave ever refused to work, he would be forced back to work with flogging, denial of food and threat of conviction. There was no relief. The British judges and magistrates took bribes from the landlords and moneylenders and punished the innocent Santhals severely.

Years of limitless exploitation, oppression and rapine left the Santhals the only option of revolt. In their language, Hool is revolt. On 30 June 1855, ten thousand Santhals representing four hundred villages assembled at Bhagnanidhi and swore to throw out all exploiters and oppressors from Santhal country and to reclaim all their land. Thirty thousand Santhals gathered to march on a deputation to the Lieutenant-Governor in Calcutta. They were disciplined and peaceful as long as their food lasted. Then they plundered the market for food at Panchketia and killed five notorious Bengali Dikus. Then Mahesh, a Police officer, ordered his police force to arrest Sidho and Kanho. But the Santhals caught Mahesh, tried him and sentenced him to death. Thus the Santhal Hool took a violent turn on 7 July 1855. It spread to various places like wildfire. Several Dikus and police officers were killed and Diku houses and markets were looted. The Dikus, Zamindars, soldiers and others were on the run. There was a fierce battle on 16 July: thirty to fifty thousand half-naked Santhals with their primitive battle-axes, swords, bows and arrows fought with fifteen thousand well-trained soldiers armed with modern powerful weapons such as cannons and guns. The British army killed the old, the women and the children without any discrimination. Some Santhals took shelter in the forest and adopted guerrilla warfare. The British Government used its ultimate weapon, martial law. Without a trace of human compassion, the British army resorted to reckless plunder, homicide, destruction, torture and humiliation of women—all a fury of horror. The Santhal rebels retreated, still fighting, from Birbhum to Santhal Pargana. An English general wrote, 'What we did was not war, it was mass murder?' (131) Thus fifty percent of the Santhals were killed.

Indian Government is as bad as the British Government and the ugly deformity of the Indian society remains the same. The play quotes various reports and news items alternately along the narration of the Santhal revolt.

TWO. According to a survey on bonded labour, or men who have been forced to sign bonds enslaving themselves for life, there are 555,000 of these in Uttar Pradesh, 467,000 in Madhya Pradesh, 325,000 in Andra Pradesh, 250,000 in Tamilnadu, 193,000 in Karnataka, 171,000 in Gujarat, 111,000 in Bihar, 105,000 in Maharashtra and 67,000 in Rajasthan. 66 percent of the bonded labour belong to the low castes, and 18 percent to the aborigines. 84 percent of the owners are high caste Hindus. Most of the bonded labourers have been driven to this pass by extreme poverty. (118)

THREE. 70 per cent of the population of West Bengal live below the poverty line, and 95 per cent below the basic nutrition line. . . . The Minister for Education has estimated an expenditure of Rupees 280 millions for the proposed Asiad to be held in Delhi in 1982. (118-19)

It is evident that the government of India has done little to improve the conditions of the poor. Though it gets elected by masses, its administration always favours the rich. It ruthlessly suppresses the movements of the people against the inhuman exploitation and oppression by the rich. It seldom protects the downtrodden.

THREE. There were 3019 cases of atrocities on the Harijans in the first nine months of 1978. 175 Harijans were killed, 129 Harijan women were raped, there were 289 cases of arson. (134)

FIVE. 13 April 1978. The police fired on a peaceful demonstration of 500 workers at the Pantnagar Agricultural University in Uttar Pradesh after blocking up the entrance and exit. 150 workers were killed, figures for the injured are not available. The dead bodies were later piled up in a sugarcane field and set on fire. (135)

FIVE. According to government reports alone, 80 prisoners were killed and 645 injured between December 1970 and April 1973 in the prisons of West Bengal and Bihar. (136)

ONE. During interrogation at the Detective Department at Lalbazar, a fifteen year old class ten schoolboy had his right hand twisted and broken, had burns from burning cigarette ends all over his body, nails from his feet torn out. There were several young men in the police lockups and prisons at this time who screamed when passing faeces with permanent wounds in their rectums made by

> rods inserted during police torture. Women prisoners too once in a month in the name of interrogation. . .
>
> (136-37)

All these instances and such incidents elucidate how social deformity and spritual deformity sustain each other. Only loveless people go to any extent in exploiting and oppressing the innocent and ignorant masses who give away their colossal power to the privileged few by taking the social deformity for granted. This creates polarization of power, leading to political deformity. These deformities thrive on the ignorance or false consciousness of the people. The play not only exposes the social deformity but also throws light on how education and mass media bring about the false consciousness among people. Education diverts the attention of the people by teaching them several irrelevant things, mass media fills their mind with stale news, business advertisements and political propaganda.

> THREE. The Chief Minister added that the situation had taken such a dangerous turn that the Executive Magistrate had no alternative to ordering a firing. The police fired nine rounds, killing and injuring . . .
>
> FOUR. The house staff and internees of the hospital struck work on Wednesday morning in protest against the attack on a senior physician in the Emergency Ward. As a result work in the outdoor department . . .
>
> FIVE. On the sixth day of the Asian Games at Bangkok, India won three gold and one silver medals. In the ten thousand metres race . . . (102)
>
> TWO. *(requesting)* Margo, your favourite soap in a new wrapping.
>
> FIVE. *(a No)* Cinivista.
>
> TWO. *(pleading)* Dial a discount! Kwality Ice creams.
>
> FIVE. *(a wavering, and then a No)* Come Alive with Nescafe.
>
> TWO. *(tempting)* Your kingsize favourite, Four Square, now in a destinctive new pack. (108)

The play quotes Rammohun, Bankimchandra and Vivekananda to show how intellectual leaders often mislead people with their wrong notions:

> RAMMOHUN. "I now conclude my Essay in offering up thanks to the Supreme Disposer of the universe, for having unexpectedly delivered this country, from the long

continued tyranny of its former Rulers, and placed it under the Government of the English, . . ." (114-15)

BANKIMCHANDRA. For we are a nation under foreign rule and we shall remain under foreign rule for many years more. (116)

Veena Noble Dass therefore comments, "The play thus attempted to expose the collaborationists' role of the Bengali middle class during the British Raj."[18] The exposure of any man to this kind of education and mass media will eventually cause the deformity of his mind. So Ella Dutta highlights this point in her introduction to *Three Plays*: "What is most important is that he is confused by the bombardment of a barrage of information, quite often contradictory, full of contrasts and perhaps even the most shattering bits of information come as stale news." (xi)

ONE learns about the exploitation, oppression and injustice that have been there in colonial and post-colonial India. He cannot remain a silent spectator any longer. So he rebels at the end of the play when the Dead Man is arrested. He urges others to react to the injustice.

ONE. Death, blood and fear rule over this land. Everyone knows what happens and will happen behind the bars of the prison. Why don't you scream? Is it still not the time? Is the time still not ripe? (138)

K. Venkata Reddy compares ONE with Indrajit, the central character of *Evam Indrajit*, another play by Sircar: "The image of the young man in *Stale News* seems to be almost an inversion of the image of Indrajit in 'Evam Indrajit.' In 'Evam Indrajit' a rebel becomes a Nirmal, a compromising inert citizen. . . . But, in *Stale News* it is the other way round. The young man, who wanted to lead a normal, routine life, becomes a rebel and revolts against the capitalistic society."[19]

The Savaras and Jatas, the tribal people living on the mountains in Srikakulam of Andhra Pradesh, revolted against the exploitation and oppression of landlords, moneylenders and government officials in 1969, more than one century after the Santhal Revolt. It was also mercilessly suppressed. Thus the play will continue to be relevant as long as the social deformity, supported by other deformities, lasts.

One Day in Ashadha by Mohan Rakesh[20] exemplifies how the social deformity weakens human love and relations. The play portrays the life of Kalidasa, the greatest ancient Indian playwright. Rakesh just makes use of a branch of research on Kalidasa to throw light on the dilemma of the present-day writer. The play makes the character of Kalidasa represent a writer who cannot resist the temptations being offered by the state and other agencies and who ignores his commitment to the people and the place that he owes his glory to. In the play, the poet succumbs to the royal allurements and betrays Mallika who loves him and who inspires him in writing great plays. Rakesh himself admits: "Therefore, poor Kalidasa has been unnecessarily dragged in, slightly demoted from his high pedestal for the sake of my dominions. But the play is about the contemporary mind."[21] He is severely criticised for this. So he explains why he like Bharati and Karnad exploits history and legend to focus on a contemporary issue: "I don't think that there's any harm in exploiting a particular character or situation in history for the sake of saying something modern, particularly if using such a character or situation would make it easier for the writer to do so."[22]

Kalidasa is an ordinary village youth. He tends the cattle of Matul, his maternal uncle. He sees and enjoys the beauty of Nature. He loves Mallika, a village lass, who shares his aesthetic sense. She becomes a part of Nature in awakening and inspiring the dormant poet in Kalidasa. She falls in love with him in whom she finds her aesthetic feelings articulated beautifully. She adores *Ritusanhar*, his first literary work whereas the rustic people fail to perceive his greatness.

One day in the month of Ashadha, Mallika spends some time with Kalidasa on the hills as usual. As it rains, she comes home. Ambika, her mother, is worried about her health while Mallika enjoys the experience of being drenched in the rain. She describes her aesthetic experience poetically:

> Soft and moist like the blue lotus, light like the wind, and picturesque like a dream. I wish I could take it into myself completely and close my eyes. . . . My whole body is saturated, Mother! The wetness of the clothes has drenched every part of me . . . oooh! The touch of heat after the biting cold!

Ambika who works hard for her beloved daughter is not at all romantic. She frankly says: "Mother's life is not made up of feelings, it's made up of work. There is much to be done in this house." She is worried about Mallika's marriage as people are not ready to accept Mallika as a bride on account of her relationship with Kalidasa.

Dantul, a gentleman of the royal family, goes hunting and hurts a fawn with his arrow. Kalidasa takes the fawn and nurses it. Dantul, in his quarrel with him for the fawn, discovers through Mallika that he is Kalidasa, the poet. He informs that the Emperor of Ujjaini wants to appoint Kalidasa the Poet Laureate. In the beginning, Kalidasa does not like to leave the village. Finally, being urged and persuaded by Mallika herself, he goes to Ujjaini. Mallika has absolute faith in him but Ambika intuitively knows the nature of Kalidasa and warns Mallika: "I understand this sort of person very well. His relationship with you is one in which you are an instrument of his self-love and pride. But you, aren't you also a living human being? Doesn't he, or don't you have a duty to yourself?" Vilom, another village youth, who loves Mallika and poetry, fails to win either. He feels jealous of Kalidasa who wins both. So he bluntly asks Kalidasa: "Won't you forget about this countryside in all the glitter of the capital?" But Kalidasa has no answer to this.

It is another day in the month of Ashadha several years later. Ambika has been ill for two years. Mallika has waited for Kalidasa all these long years but in vain. Nikshep, the common friend of Mallika and Kalidasa, is shocked by the unexpected behaviour of Kalidasa. He says to Mallika: "But I have heard that he married the Gupta Princess and reminds her of those days, . . . When he was living here he vowed that he would never marry." But Mallika does not blame him. Now, she works hard as her mother did previously. Rangini and Sangini, the ladies from the royal court, visit Mallika's house to discover what has made Kalidasa a great poet. But they are intoxicated with the royal pomp and cannot understand that the innocent Mallika living in her humble home can inspire marvellous poetry in Kalidasa. Then Anunasik and Anuswar, the two gentlemen of the royal court, come to make the place tidy for the visit of the Queen. Later Priyangumanjari, the Queen comes and says to Mallika: "I said that I want to take the atmosphere of this place with me. I do not want him to feel the absence of this place. His missing it is often very harmful." Then she offers to get her house renovated and to get her married to either of the two gentlemen. But Mallika does not accept it and Ambika is thoroughly annoyed by the indifference of her daughter to herself. The Queen leaves and Vilom comes. Kalidasa comes to the village but does not visit Mallika. Vilom frankly says, 'Friendship exists between equals.' Now Kalidasa is the Governor of Kashmir. He forgets Mallika as Dushyanta betrays Shakuntala in *Abhijnanashakuntalam*, the famous play of Kalidasa.

It is again another day in the month of Ashadha after several more years. Matul commiserates with Mallika. He realizes that wealth upsets one's physical and mental health. He confesses:

> Had I known I was going to break my leg inside the royal palace, I never would have left the village. While I was gone they made the floor of my house here so slippery that I can't take a sure step.

> They made it of marble slabs which won't grip my feet. The earthen floor was better. Now, even though I live in that house, I am homeless.

After Matul leaves, Kalidasa comes. He sees the destitution of Mallika. He is overcome by the feelings of deep remorse. He admits his guilt:

> I have thought about myself many times, Mallika, and frequently decided that Ambika was right. . . . Why did I hesitate to go away from here? One reason was that I wasn't confident of myself. I did not know how I would react to the honour and fame after a life of poverty and dishonour. I was afraid that it would overwhelm me and change the direction of my life. This fear was not unfounded.

He could not stand the travails of administrative responsibilities any longer and fled in disguise. He feels ashamed to know how deeply Mallika has loved him all these years. In spite of her penury, she has saved money to buy all the literary works of Kalidasa. And she has bought a bundle of palm leaves for Kalidasa to write on another great literary work. He finds some stains of her tears and sweat on the leaves. He considers that it is indeed a great literary work that she has written in tears.

Kalidasa confesses that the royal comforts have not added anything to his poetic endeavour:

> People think that living in that life and atmosphere I have written a great deal. But I know that while living there I wrote nothing. Whatever I wrote was a recollection of life here. The Himalayas are the backdrop for 'Kumarasambhav' and you are the austere Uma. The pain of the yaksha in 'Meghdut' is the pain I felt at being separated from you and the pain of the yaksha's wife is your pain, though I imagined myself here and you in Ujjaini. You were before me in the form of Shakuntala. Whenever I made an effort to write I repeated the tale of our lives over and over. If I turned away from this and tried to write, the works were lifeless.

He later learns that Mallika has accepted Vilom for her survival. Moreover she has borne him a child. So Kalidasa cannot share life with Mallika. He thinks that time wins the struggle between herself and desire. So he leaves. Mallika calls him but he is already gone. She then takes her child and caresses her gently.

The social deformity distorts our thinking and perception. Our society appears to be made of a few superior people and a vast majority of inferior people. But we do not realize that superiority and inferiority which are often or always defined wrongly are actually psycho-culturally programmed. Kalidasa and Vilom are equally great. The difference in their sensibilities reflects the different ways that they have been brought up. So, Kalidasa becomes a successful poet while Vilom remains a peasant. Mallika is a victim of cultural prejudices; so she runs after Kalidasa who runs after royal honours. She does not love Vilom who offers to marry her. She cannot perceive the tenderness of his heart hidden under his rough behaviour. Vilom lives with Mallika who is forced to accept him by poverty. All of them ruin their life by trying to scramble up the ladder of social hierarchy. The play while depicting the inner conflict of Kalidasa deflates the concept of 'superman.' Vivek Dutta Jha aptly puts it: "In our society, from the very beginning, we have had a tendency to consider a great thinker, preacher or an artist as a superman: . . . We are unable to accept them as having human weaknesses. But here the writer has tried to break this old illusion by bringing before us a character like Kalidasa with all the human weaknesses."[23] Certain ideas and modes of behaviour get psycho-culturally fixed firmly in the mind of everybody and it is almost impossible for anybody to get freed from them. It is no use blaming and criticising one. Only a new-born baby is free from these until the psycho-cultural programming begins. So, it is in a way symbolic that Mallika in the end caresses her baby instead of running after Kalidasa.

The social deformity manifests itself in various forms depending on the kind of hierarchy such as economic, ethical and cultural. It is logical and perhaps just for anybody to covet the highest rung in the social hierarchy. It is equally natural for the people to compete for the highest rung and to do anything to reach their coveted goal. The people of higher rungs enjoy several privileges at the cost of the people of lower rungs. People take all this for granted. Tendulkar's *Vultures* shows how some people in their mad scramble to the top do not mind becoming vultures, the birds of prey, which symbolize ruthless exploitation. Hari Pitale cheats his own brother in business and becomes rich. His children absorb his exploitative culture. So, they bully their own father to get them the money deposited in his name in a bank. Ramakant and Umakant break the leg of their own sister Manik to prevent her from spoiling their plan of blackmailing the Raja of Hondur, her lover, for money. They mercilessly cause abortion to her when they learn that he is dead. They look down upon their servants and workers and grudge to pay them wages. The people of lower rungs accept their inferiority which is in fact psycho-culturally programmed. They seldom realize their potential of becoming as great as the so-called superior people. In

Karnad's *Hayavadana*, Kapila, the blacksmith, sits down on the floor while his Brahmin friend, Devadatta, sits on a chair. He does not sit on the chair even when Devadatta requests him to do so. Thus, most of the people give away their power to the privileged few by accepting the hierarchy which has, therefore, survived all the reforms and revolutions.

Social deformity is thus illustrated in its various aspects in Karnad's *Tale-Danda*, Sircar's *Stale News* and Rakesh's *One Day in Ashadha*. The ugly face of the caste system in India is exposed in *Tale-Danda*. Most of the people accept it and observe the customs that sustain it. Moreover state protects it with military force. Basavanna is betrayed by his own followers in his ideal struggle to eradicate the caste system gradually. Consequently, not only does Basavanna's movement fail but also his followers emerge as a new caste after a few hundred years. *Stale News* elaborately presents several instances of ruthles exploitation and oppression in India during pre- and post-Independence periods. Sircar juxtaposes them and successfully proves that Indian Government is as bad as the British Government. The struggles of the people against exploitation and oppression like the Santhal Revolt are mercilessly repressed by military forces. The Santhal revolt meets with the same fate as the movement of *sharanas*. *One Day in Ashadha* shows how social deformity destroys human love. Kalidasa is tempted by royal luxuries. Therefore he betrays Mallika, the poor village lass who has inspired him to write his masterpieces and marries the princess. Thus Karnad, Sircar and Rakesh expose the evil effects of social deformity at cultural, social and psychological levels.

NOTES

1. J. Bruce Long, 'Life out of Death,' *Hinduism*, ed. Bardwell L. Smith (Leiden: E.J. Brill, 1982) 172.
2. Cluade M. Steiner, *Scripts People Live* (New York: Bantam, 1980) 186.
3. Marx and Engels, *Manifesto of the Communist Party* (Moscow: Progress Publishers, 1977) 64.
4. Brahmins are called *Bhusuras* (Gods on earth) in Sanskrit.
5. *Hindu Customs and their Origins* (Delhi: Low Price Publications, 1993) 122.
6. *Dr. Babasaheb Ambedkar: Writings and Speeches* (Bombay: Government of Maharashtra, 1987) 67.
7. Qtd. Ambedkar, p. 418.

8. Lord Rama beheaded Shambuka, a shudra, for reading Vedas.
9. Venkatesan, "Caste Crimes," *Frontline*, July 29, 1994, 104. (This can be illustrated by the incident reported by Venkatesan in *Frontline*. Subhash, a shudra boy of twelve years, allegedly broke the glass shell of 'akhand jyoti' on 28 May 1994 in Jaitsar, a village of Rajasthan. For not allowing him to be caught, Prakash Kaur, his mother, was most inhumanly punished. She was stripped naked, dragged with her legs tied around the Durga Temple and beaten with sticks all the time by upper caste men and one of them allegedly pushed hard a stick into her genitals. Then her head was tonsured, her face was blackened and she was paraded on a donkey in the market. Hot water and then kerosene were poured down into her mouth. She could not survive the heinous torture and died. This is only one of the incidents that often happen throughout India).
10. Girish Karnad, *Tale-Danda* (Delhi: Ravi Dayal Publisher, 1993) 14.
11. Linga is the holy phallic symbol of Lord Shiva.
12. "Where is the tradition?" (Interview), *Frontline*, September 25, 1992, 76.
13. *Loc. cit.*
14. *Loc. cit.*
15. Qtd. Gowri Ramnarayan, "The endless road" *Frontline*, August 28, 1992, 75.
16. "Badal Sircar's Third Theatre," Diss., S.K. University, 1993, Footnote 5, 62.
17. Badal Sircar, *Stale News* trans. Samik Bandyopadhyay, *Three Plays*, (Calcutta: Seagull Books, 1985) 94-95.
18. *Modern Indian Drama in English Translation* (New Delhi, 1988) 78.
19. "India's Barefoot Playwright, Badal Sircar," *Critical Studies in Commonwealth Literature* (New Delhi: Prestige, 1994) 135.
20. Mohan Rakesh, *One Day in Ashadha*, trans. Sarah K. Ensley, *Enact*, Aug.-Sept., 1969, no page.
21. Interview with Mohan Rakesh, *A Journal of South Asian Literature*, Vol. IX, No. 2 & 3, Fall & Winter 1973, 32.
22. Rakesh, 33.
23. "Mohan Rakesh and his Plays," Creative Agencies, 1 *Enact*, Jan.-Feb. 1973, no page.

Political Deformity: Karnad's *Tughlaq*, Tendulkar's *Ghasiram Kotwal* and Sircar's *That Other History*

> But for that I'll have to admit I've been wrong all these years. And I know I haven't. I have something to give, something to teach, which may open the eyes of history, but I have to do it within this life. I've got to make them listen to me before I lose even that!
>
> *Tughlaq*

In primitive times, human beings felt that they were powerless and inferior because they, having become aware of their own identity, alienated themselves from Nature. They have been striving to become powerful and superior since then. As civilization progressed, the alienation entered human society and caused various divisions of it. And the urge to be more powerful than one another hierarchized those divisions. This has made the society pyramidical where the few at the top usurp the great power of the masses at the bottom. This has become possible and usual because the people give away their power by taking the hierarchized society for granted. As the higher rungs of the hierarchized society are endowed with greater power in addition to the greater privileges, people struggle hard to scramble up the ladder of power. In this, some go up while some go down. The family trains children in this struggle for power.

It is very interesting to see how a human child, like its primitive ancestors, also feels powerless when it becomes conscious of itself and its environment. Adler, a neo-Freudian, talks about the universal feeling of inferiority:

> The child, by virtue of his small size and helplessness, inevitably considers himself inferior to the adult figures in his environment. Parents who neglect, ridicule, or lack tenderness in their dealings with the child often accentuate his feeling of being subordinate. The mother plays an especially crucial part in this process, for by treating him lightly or by pampering and overprotecting him she

hinders the acquisition of social skills. The family constellation also serves to intensify inferiority feelings.[1]

Augusto Boal, the originator of the theatre of the oppressed, says: "Sometimes you can oppress by giving, you can oppress through tenderness, you can oppress through suffering."[2] He makes it clear that people are oppressed not only through cruetly but also through pity. As Adler points out, parents oppress their children in these two ways and make them powerless.

Karpman, a Transactional Analyst, identifies three roles in this situation of oppression: Rescuer, Persecutor and Victim. According to him, these roles form Drama Triangle which is called Rescue Triangle by Steiner. He explains: "The Rescue triangle is an efficient training ground for the acceptance of hierarchies of power in which every person is one-up to some and one-down to other." He further argues that "having been in a powerless position, we make ourselves feel better by taking, and assuming power over others as Rescuers or Persecutors."[3]

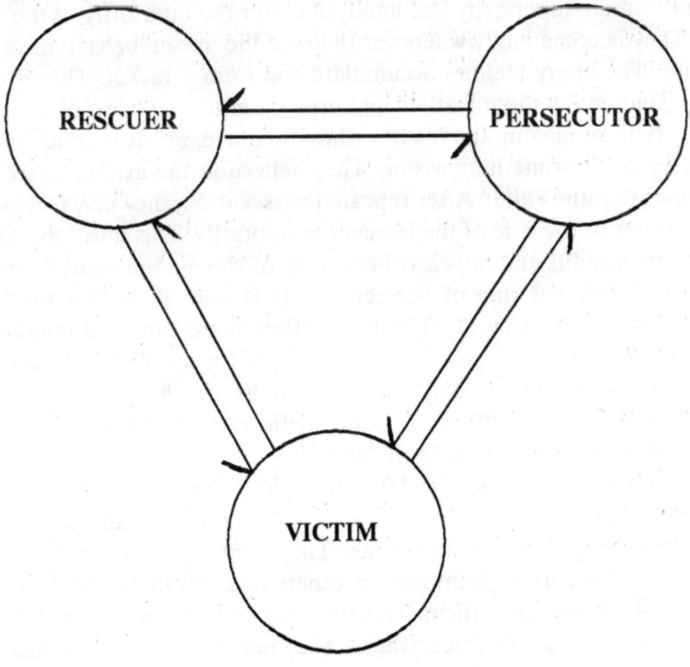

KARPMAN DRAMA TRIANGLE

Rescuers feel that they are superior to the Victim and that the latter is helpless and hopeless without their rescuing him, or her. They conveniently ignore the inherent ability of everyone to help himself or herself. They feel "not ok" and guilty about their superiority whenever they see the helplessness of the Victims. These feelings of guilt accumulate and form a racket. They obsess their mind, make them restless and urge them to make use of their superiority in rescuing the Victim. For this, they sacrifice their own interests and comforts. They always fail in improving the conditions of the Victim who never tries to help himself or herself and who passively accepts the rescuing. They are never thanked for their rescuing. Moreover, they find themselves exploited and thus persecuted by the Victim. This leads to a racket of feelings of anger and they persecute the Victim. As soon as these feelings are spent, they return to their favourite role of rescuing as they start feeling guilty for having persecuted the Victim. A typical Rescuer chooses such a profession as allows him or her to play the role; so he or she becomes a leader, a teacher, a preacher, a social worker or an officer.

Persecutors also feel that they are superior to the Victim. They feel proud of their superiority and annoyed about the inferiority of the Victim. They become angry whenever they see the 'mean' behaviour of the Victim. The angry feelings accumulate and form a racket. They obsess their mind, make them restless and urge them to make use of their superiority in punishing the Victim who, of course, behaves complementarily by doing something wrong. They believe in the axiom, 'spare the rod and spoil the child.' After repeated persecution, they may feel guilty and so shift to the role of the Rescuer temporarily. This invariably leads to the ungrateful and hopeless behaviour of the Victim which justifies only their original role of persecuting. It is also likely that the Persecutor is punished by the Victim and thus there can be a temporary reversal of roles. A typical Persecutor opts for such a profession as enables him or her to play the role; so he or she becomes a disciplinarian, a strict officer, a police officer, a public prosecutor, a criminal, a jailor or a military officer.

Victims feel that they are inferior to their Rescuer and Persecutor. They feel powerless. They look forward to being rescued and persecuted by others. They never see any choice. They remain dependent on others or chance. They look pliant and let others take advantage of them, exploit them or victimize them. They then send verbal or non-verbal signals to the Rescuer to rescue them. They never try to help themselves but enjoy being rescued. They resent being belittled by the Rescuer whom they, therefore, never thank for their help. Moreover, they persecute the Rescuer by exploiting the rescuing, by demanding more rescuing, by being ungrateful and by remaining unimproved. On the other hand, they look flaccid and succumb to doing wrong things and making mistakes repeatedly. Thus, they invite the attention of their Persecutor who punishes them sufficiently. A typical Victim selects the professions of the lower rungs so as to play his or her role.

People play their favourite roles most of the time; yet they shift to other roles temporarily. A person may play different roles in different situations. Drama Triangle has been socio-culturally accepted and perpetuated. God's saving his devotee from the demon form the inner core of several myths. Almost every story contains three major roles—hero, villain and victim. The shifting of roles is not uncommon. This can be illustrated by the myth of Bhasmasura: Lord Shiva is pleased with the devotion of his devotee, Bhasmasura and grants him the boon that he asked for. So, Bhasmasura gets the power of reducing anybody to ashes by placing his palm on his head. He is so curious to test the power of the boon that he runs after Lord Shiva to test it on Him. Lord Vishnu, in the guise of a beautiful lady, diverts Bhasmasura and saves Shiva. Here, Lord Shiva, the Rescuer, becomes the Victim whereas Bhasmasura, the Victim, becomes his Persecutor.

In a typical family, Father plays the Persecutor and Mother the Rescuer while children are Victims. When Father hurts children, Mother rescues them. Then, Father becomes her Victim as she persecutes him for hurting children. Later, she becomes the Victim of children who exploit her kindness and they rescue Mother when Father hurts her. When they grow up, they either rescue or persecute their old parents. Talking about the shifting of roles, Steiner points out: "Every Rescuer-Victim transaction will eventually result in a Persecutor-Victim transaction" (182) The concept of Drama Triangle which explains political deformity is illustrated in Karnad's *Tughlaq*, Tendulkar's *Ghasiram Kotwal* and Sircar's *That Other History*.

In *Tughlaq*, not only the protagonist but also other characters are involved in Drama Triangle by playing different roles according to the situation. Even in the beginning, an old Muslim persecutes Muhammad-bin-Tughlaq whom a Muslim youth rescues:

> OLD MAN: God, what's this country coming to!
> YOUNG MAN: What are you worried about, grandfather? The country's in perfectly safe hands—safer than any you've seen before.[4]

The dialogue runs into five pages in this way. Muhammad who plays the Rescuer effects certain reforms which he thinks will help his people (his

Victims). One of the reforms is the removal of jizia tax that the previous Muslim kings urged non-Muslims to pay. But a Hindu, instead of being grateful to the Sultan, criticises him. The Muslim therefore calls him 'Ungrateful wretch.'

Muhammad, as a typical Rescuer thinks that his people are helpless and miserable. He feels that he alone can rescue them from their misery and that other kings, who are not so enlightened as he, could not do it:

MUHAMMAD:	No, really. Suppose I die in the battle. What of it? Why should I waste my last few days worrying? I am not worried about my enemies. I'm only worried about my people.
STEP-MOTHER:	Pompous ass! As though other kings did not do it.
MUHAMMAD:	No, they didn't. (11)

He forgoes his physical comforts such as sleep and marital bliss and even his mental peace in order to rescue his people. He wants to build an ideal kingdom for his people.

> MUHAMMAD (theatrical): I pray to the Almighty to save me from sleep. . . . Then again I want to climb up, upto the tallest tree in the world, and call out to my people: 'Come, my people, I am waiting for you. Confide in me your worries. Let me share your joys. Let's laugh and cry together and then let's pray. . . . Come! I am waiting to embrace you all!' But then how can I spread my branches in the stars while the roots have yet to find their hold in the earth? I wish I could believe in recurring births like the Hindu but I have only one life, one body, and my hopes, my people, my God are all fighting for it. Tell me, how dare I waste my time by sleeping? And don't tell me to go and get married and breed a family because I won't sleep. (10)

Even his step-mother says, "he works so hard for the people. He doesn't even go to bed these days." (17) He pleads with the Amirs of Delhi to cooperate with him in realizing his ideal:

> I have hopes of building a new future for India and I need your support for that. If you don't understand me, ask me to explain myself and I'll do it. If you don't understand my explanations, bear with me in patience until I can show you the results. But please

don't let me down, I beg you. I'll kneel before you if you wish but please don't let go off my hand. (40)

This idealism is a common feature of typical Rescuers. Karnad himself finds a parallel between Muhammad and Nehru: "And I felt in the early sixties India had also come very far in the same direction—the twenty-year period seemed to me very much a striking parallel."[5] Jawaharlal Nehru indeed shares the same idealism as that of Muhammad to build modern India and he worked hard, foregoing his sleep and other comforts. Aparna Dharwadker considers this the first phase of Muhammad's rule and comments on his idealism: "The first is the untenability of the idealistic and visionary politics that Nehru and Mahatma Gandhi practiced as national leaders and valorized in their respective meditations on political action—*The Discovery of India* and *The Story of my Experiments with Truth*."[6]

Muhammad feels that he is far superior to any other in his enlightenment and idealism. Indeed he is a great scholar and thinker. He thinks that whatever he does is right. He justifies his actions to Imam-ud-din in a scholarly manner:

> I still remember the days when I read the Greeks—Sukrat who took poison so he could give the world the drink of gods, Aflatoon who condemned poets and wrote incomparably beautiful poetry himself—and I can still feel the thrill with which I found a new world I had not found in the Arabs or even the Koran. They tore me into shreds. And to be whole now, I shall have to kill the part of me which sang to them. And my kingdom too is what I am—torn into pieces by visions whose validity I can't deny. You are asking me to make myself complete by killing the Greek in me and you propose to unify my people by denying the visions which led Zarathustra or the Buddha.[7] (21)

Imam-ud-din agrees, 'you are a learned man' and tells him that his people cannot be so idealistic. Muhammad does not accept any alternative to his idealistic decisions. As a typical Rescuer, he feels guilty, deeply guilty, when he cannot make use of his superiority in rescuing his people and when he persecutes people for not accepting and observing his ideals:

> BARANI: It's as your Majesty said. . . . He says the Sultan is a disgrace to Islam.
>
> MUHAMMAD: That's all ? I could find worse faults in me. What else? (13)

Ratan Singh says to Shihab-ud-din about Muhammad: "I have never seen an honest scoundrel like your Sultan. He murders a man calmly and then actually enjoys the feeling of guilt." (28) As a racket of guilty feelings develop, it urges him to rescue somebody. Muhammad therefore tries to do what he thinks is good for his people without their asking for it. Since rescuing is not realistic, it never succeeds in reaching the goal. Usually wrong people exploit his reforms and remain ungrateful to him. Aziz represents those people in the play.

The Sultan announces equality of justice to all on the second anniversary of his coronation. He adds that people may file a suit against the Sultan himself for the misbehaviour of his officers. Aziz tells Aazam, his friend, how he exploited this:

AZIZ: There's no future in being a dhobi these days. So I did a bit of thinking. There's a Brahmin called Vishnu Prasad whose land had been confiscated recently. I shaved my head and went to him. I said I would buy the land.

AAZAM: The land was confiscated, wasn't it?

AZIZ: Exactly, that's what he said too. But I said, 'Never mind about that,' so he sold me the land—backdating the contract. And I filed my suit. Well, here I am. Five hundred silver dinars for nothing, and a job in His Merciful Majesty's own Civil Service. (7-8)

But Muhammad does not know this and thinks that he has succeeded in implementing the equality. He is overwhelmed by this mythical success and addresses the people:

> My beloved people, you have heard the judgement of the Kazi and seen for yourselves how justice works in my kingdom—without any consideration of might or weakness, religion or creed. May this moment burn bright and light up our path towards greater justice, equality, progress and peace—not just peace but a more purposeful life. (3)

Encouraged by this imaginary success of his idealism, he announces the shift of the capital from Delhi to Daulatabad. He then explains how the shift will benefit their country in several ways.

Aziz is ever ready to exploit every reform of Muhammad. He mercilessly takes bribes from the people on their way to Daulatabad for small concessions as he is an officer. When the Sultan introduces copper coins, he at once starts minting counterfeit coins. Later every Hindu home becomes a domestic mint. Then, Aziz gets silver dinars for his copper coins as the Sultan starts giving silver dinars in exchange for copper coins. He buys land very cheaply and collects the state subsidy for farmers. As it is discovered, he flees to the hills and becomes a robber. Finally, the desperate Sultan seeks the religious help from Ghiyas-ud-din. Aziz assassinates Ghiyas-ud-din and impersonates him. Then, he lands in the royal palace and leads the prayer. When his friend Aazam gets killed, Muhammad discovers the impersonation. He learns how Aziz has exploited all his reforms. Then he makes him an officer in the Deccan army as a punishment for his crimes. He finds his mirror image, his alter ego, in Aziz. While Muhammad is a Rescuer, Aziz is a Persecutor. How Aziz enlightens Aazam throws light on his contemptible attitude towards the society. For instance, he says:

> If you remain virtuous throughout your life no one will say a good thing about you because they won't need to. But start stealing—and they'll say: 'What a nice boy he was! But he's ruined now. . . . ' Then kill and they will beat their breasts and say: 'Heavens! He was only a petty thief all these days. Never hurt any one. But alas!' Then rape a woman and the chorus will go into hallelujahs: 'He was a saint, a real saint and look at him now.' (57)

Muhammad gets enraged when anybody tries to impede his ideals. He shifts to the role of Persecutor and goes to any extent to remove obstacles in the path of his ideals. First, he gets his own father and brother killed at prayer in an accident contrived by him. He himself admits it: "I killed them—yes—but I killed them for an ideal." (65) Muhammad, during the second year of his rule, faces two problems: Imam-ud-din condemns anti-Islam policies of Muhammad very eloquently at various places and Ain-ul-Mulk, whom Muhammad made the governor of Avadh, wages a war against him. He, with the help of Najib, hatches a plot to solve both the problems with one stroke. He sends Imam-ud-din to Ain-ul-Mulk as his emissary on peace mission to avert the bloodbath. Imam-ud-din, dressed in royal costumes, rides the royal elephant. He looks like the Sultan himself. When he is about to speak something, the Sultan army sounds the trumpet. The battle is on. Imam-ud-din is killed by Ain-ul-Mulk before he understands the situation. Ain-ul-Mulk realizes his mistake and seeks the protection of the Sultan against the wrath of Muslims. Muhammad forgives him. He gets the Amirs of Delhi killed by Hindu soliders during prayer as they try to kill him. After prayer, he kills Shihab-ud-din who joins hands with the Amirs in the plot. After the shifting of the capital to Daulatabad, he gets several people killed on suspicion. His Step-Mother thinks that Najib misleads him so she gets Najib killed. Muhammad is enraged by this and gets her stoned to death. This shift of roles by him from the Rescuer to the Persecutor can be illustrated by his own words: "I was too soft, I can see that now. They'll only understand the whip." (44)

Aparna Dharwadker considers this the second phase resembling the rule of Indira Gandhi and others in contrast with the first phase resembling the rule of Nehru, her father. She writes:

> The analogies with Mahatma Gandhi and Nehru thus foreground the more or less well-intentioned idealism of Tughlaq-Barani in the play's first half and suppress the cruelty, repressiveness, and cunning of Tughlaq-Aziz in the second. The analogies with Indira Gandhi (and her political successors) reverse the emphasis and bring the two halves of the play together, because what Romesh Thapar calls her 'mercurial, manipulative, conspirational, brilliant' style of leadership replicates the contradictions and tensions within Tughlaq to an extra ordinary extent. (52-53)

Muhammad's life and rule cannot be divided into two different successive phases. Actually Muhammad is basically a Rescuer and often shifts to the role of the Persecutor as a part of his rescuing the people or country. His rescuing follows his persecution. He announces equality of justice after killing his father and brother. He forgives Ain-ul-Mulk and grants his wish after getting Imam-ud-din killed. He arranges all possible facilities for the people to travel from Delhi to Daulatabad after the assassination of the Amirs and Shihab-ud-din. He gives people silver dinars in exchange for copper coins which accumulate in cart-loads in his rose garden after his merciless persecution of certain people on suspicion. His profound feelings of guilt and spiritual agony can be seen in his appeal to God who he considers is the Supreme Rescuer:

> God! God in Heaven, please help me. Please don't let go off my hand. My skin drips with blood and I don't know how much of it is mine and how much of others. I started in your path, Lord, why am I wandering naked in the desert now? I started in search of you. Why am I become a pig rolling in this gory mud? Raise me. Clean me. Cover me with your Infinite Mercy. I can only clutch at the hem of your cloak with my bloody fingers and plead. I can only beg—have pity on me. (67)

He revives prayer which he banned because the Amirs tried to kill him at prayer. He admits his fault in introducing copper coins and finally in shifting the capital. He confesses this to Barani: "There is only one place to go back to now. Delhi. Back to Delhi, Barani, I have to get back to Delhi with my people." (84) That is why Aparna Dharwadker compares Muhammed to Mrs. Gandhi: "In the political mythology of the nation Mrs. Gandhi appears both as demon and goddess, emasculating widow and nurturing mother. . . . But she is closest to Karnad's protagonist in her propensity for choosing evil out of a compulsion to act for the nation and in the self-destructiveness of her authoritarianism." (53) The images of god and demon refer to the roles of the Rescuer and the Persecutor.

Other characters also play their favourite roles. Step-Mother persecutes Najib in order to rescue her son from his bad influence. Sheik Imam-ud-din first persecutes Muhammad in order to rescue Muslims from his anti-Islam rule. Later he becomes the Sultan's Rescuer by agreeing to be his emissary to Ain-ul-Mulk but turns out to be the Victim by getting killed. Shihab-ud-din at first is the Rescuer of the Sultan as he looks after the administration when the latter goes to the war against Ain-ul-Mulk. Later, he becomes his Persecutor by being convinced by Ratan Singh, his friend, to join hands with the Amirs in the plot against the Sultan. Finally, he shifts to the role of Victim by being stabbed mercilessly by the Sultan. Ain-ul-Mulk rescues Muhammad by suppressing the rebellion in Avadh; then, he persecutes the latter by waging a war against him; finally, he becomes the Victim to be saved by the latter from the wrath of Muslims because of his killing Sheik Imam-ud-din by mistake. Barani, finally, perceives the lethality of the situation, takes the permission of the sultan and leaves the capital.

People get involved in Drama Triangle and play dangerous games in order to feel powerful and important. Muhammad is no exception to this. Aparna Dharwadker rightly observes: "Tughlaqu's madness and tyranny—the only qualities his subjects attribute to him—are thus forms of powerlessness posing as power." (52) M.K. Naik compares Karnad's *Tughlaq* with Camus's *Caligula* and finds the ultimate failure of power common to both of them. Veena Noble Dass discusses the symbolism of the play and observes: "The game of chess is also an important symbol, symbolising as it does the political gambles Tughlaq's entire career turns out to be."[8] Most of the critics attributed the fiasco of Muhammad to his idealism. U.R. Anantha Murthy in his introduction to the play recognises the two opposite roles played by Muhammad and others: "Both Tughlaq and his enemies initially appear to be idealists; yet, in the pursuit of the ideal, they perpetrate the opposite." (ix) The power games in the play, therefore, reveal that every Rescuer-Victim transaction eventually becomes a Persecutor-Victim transaction.

While we find the Rescuer in Karnad's *Tughlaq*, we can find the Persecutor in Tendulkar's *Ghasiram Kotwal* though there is shifting of roles in both the plays. Ghasiram is greatly hurt and humiliated by the people of Poona. So, he wants to avenge this on them, but he feels powerless. He wants to get power by becoming the Kotwal of the city. Steiner's explanation of the roles elucidates this situation:

> Being a Rescuer gives us the feeling of being one-up, and this is its only pleasure—it does remove us from the Victim, one-down role. We can also get one-up by becoming Persecutors, but this role is not sanctioned as fully. Generally to be a Persecutor we have to have some sort of official title or badge which legitimizes our persecution. (183)

Like *Tughlaq*, this play is based on history and the focus is on the contemporary political scene rather than history. It is set in the late eighteenth century history of Maharashtra when Balaji Janardan Bhanu was the chief administrator (Nana Phadnavis). People criticised him bitterly on the charge that the play was anti-Brahmin and that it distorted the history. In an author's note, Tendulkar says:

> This is not a historical play. It is a story, in prose, verse, music and dance set in a historical era. Ghasirams are creations of socio-political forces which know no barriers of time and place. Although based on a historical legend, I have no intention of commentary on the morals, or lack of them, of the Peshwa, Nana Phadnavis or Ghasiram.[9]

Commenting on the form and the theme of the play, Girish Karnad explains clearly the contemporary relevance of the play in the introduction to his three plays:

> In his *Ghasiram Kotwal*, Tendulkar uses *Dashavatara*, a traditional semiclassical form, to investigate a contemporary political problem, the emergence of 'demons' in public. These demons are initially created by political leaders for the purposes of their own power games, but ultimately go out of control and threaten to destroy their own creators. It is a theme recurrent in Indian mythology: the demon made indestructible by the boon of gods and then turning on the gods themselves. (A decade after the play

> was written, in Punjab, Sant Bhindranwale and Mrs. Indira Gandhi seemed to be re-enacting the theme in real life in horrifying detail.)[10]

Therefore, unless we understand the power game in the play we are likely to miss the theme and to agree with Veena Noble Dass who says that "the central weakness of the play is that Ghasiram has been provided with too explicit reason for his conversion from man to monster." (113)

Ghasiram Savaldas is a poor Brahman from Kanauj. He, with his wife and daughter, comes to Poona for livelihood. Since he gets no noble employment to suit his caste, he becomes a servant in courtesan Gulabi's house. In addition to the housework that he does for her, he also sings and dances when people come to enjoy her erotic songs and dances. Once, Nana Phadnavis visits Gulabi. He sprains his ankle during the dance. Then, Ghasiram holds his hurt foot in his hands and says: "In my hands has fallen grace! All here envy me my place!" Nana feels flattered and pleased and offers him a necklace of pearls and leaves. Gulabi snatches the necklace from him and sends him out with the help of her thugs. Ghasiram feels hurt and insulted. Thus, Gulabi who once rescues Ghasiram persecutes him later and Ghasiram who remains in the position of the Victim feels helpless and powerless.

Ghasiram then goes out. He feels tired and hungry. When Peshwa arranges a great feast in honour of Brahmans, he also goes there. But the soldiers do not let him in. Meanwhile a Brahman whose money, given by Peshwa, is stolen yells that some thief has stolen his money. The soldiers beat Ghasiram severely. Then, Nana comes and says that the thief is gone. Brahmans go running after Nana who gives them coins. The soldiers put Ghasiram in prison on the charge of theft though Nana says that he is not the thief. After some time, a soldier throws him out and orders him to leave Poona on pain of death. Then Brahmans, Brahman women, Gulabi, the Maratha lovers and others look down upon Ghasiram. So he feels immensely humiliated and tormented. In his fury, he says:

> But I'll come back. I'll come back to Poona. I'll show my strength. It will cost you! Your good days are gone! . . . I'll come back like a boar and I'll stay as a devil. I'll make pigs of all of you. I'll make this Poona a kingdom of pigs. Then I'll be Ghasiram again, the son of Savaldas once more. (17)

Now he looks for the best way to get enough power to persecute the people of Poona.

Some people go to the temple of Lord Ganesh. A Haridasa narrates a religious tale through song and dance. Meanwhile Nana comes and people pay their reverence to him. They listen to the tale while he ogles the women. When the tale is over, people bow to the Haridasa and leave one by one. At last, a pretty lass prays to Ganesh when Nana gets all the doors closed. He puts his hand on her and lustfully says: "All your dreams, this Nana will fulfill." (18) She expresses her fear of being seen and steals away. He runs after her and holds a servant by mistake. Then he urges the servant to go and find her: "If she is not found, no one will keep his head! Our grandeur's gone if she's not had. We tell you, if she is found, then this Nine Court Nana will conquer Hindustan! What a bosom! Buds just blossoming. . . . We'll squeeze them like this." (20)

People know that even Peshwa obeys whatever Nana says. Nana is very powerful and the fear of Nana grows day by day. Ghasiram who is in the guise of the servant brings the girl, none but his own daughter, Gauri and sends her to Nana. He seeks power through his daughter. "Now he's in my hands . . . I've given my beloved daughter in the jaws of the wolf." (22) Nana who enjoys erotic pleasure with Gauri once wants her again and again. Ghasiram blackmails him on this and urges him to make him the Kotwal of Poona. Nana issues the order making Ghasiram the Kotwal of Poona. Samik in the introduction comments, "Tendulkar suggests the sexuality implicit in power in the brilliant innuendo that caps the situation: 'our grandeur's gone if she's not had.' Nana needs Ghasiram. And Ghasiram needs Nana." (v) Thus Nana and Ghasiram rescue each other.

Ghasiram starts persecuting the people of Poona who have humiliated him before and who also happen to be the enemies of Nana. Nana is happy that Ghasiram is doing what he himself wants to do.

> Go, Ghashya, old bastard. We made you. We made you Kotwal. Raise hell if you wish. But you don't know the ways of this Nana. This time, there are two bullets in this gun. With the first one, we'll fell your luscious daughter. But with the second we will make the city of Poona dance. Ghashya, child, you're a foreigner. I have put you on Poona's back. Why? As a countercheck to all those conspirators. You'll not be able to join them; they'll never trust you even if you do. . . . What'll happen is that our misdeeds will be credited to your account. We do; our Kotwal pays. (24-25)

Samik explains how Nana exercises his power safely through Ghasiram and how this reflects the contemporary political scene in India.

> Like ceremony, both religious and secular, the deceptions of deputation constitute yet another device of power. The real power uses the masks of deputation to mediate the exercise of power, to hide from the victims the real face of power so that all resistance is effectively deflected. Intermediate democratic institutions, or the paraphernalia of bureaucracy, too often regarded as repositories of at least executive power, are more often than not masks or mediations that veil the actual exercise of power and hide the perpetrator from the eyes of the victim. (vi)

The role of Nana in the power game can be understood clearly through the Game Pentagon proposed by Oswald Summerton, an Australian Transactional Analyst.[11] He adds two more roles, the Spectator and the Stage-Manager, to the three roles of the Drama Triangle. While Peshwa remains the Spectator, Nana becomes the Stage-Manager, managing the power game in which Ghasiram who persecutes the people of Poona ruthlessly finally ends up as their Victim by being mercilessly humiliated and murdered by them.

Ghasiram as a typical Persecutor feels that he is superior to his Victims (the people of Poona). So he cannot tolerate being victimized by the inferior people whom he calls pigs. The Brahmans of Poona once enjoyed the erotic pleasure with courtesans while their wives enjoyed the company of Maratha lovers and courtesans like Gulabi earned great wealth by offering the Brahmans erotic experience. All this is stopped with immediate effect. Everybody has to take the permission of Ghasiram to do anything out of routine. Sutradhar narrates:

> Ghasiram Kotwal says to kill a pig, to do an abortion, to be a pimp, to commit a misdemeanour, to steal, to live with one's divorced wife, to remarry if one's husband is alive, to hide one's caste, to use counterfeit coins, to commit suicide, without a permit, is a sin. A good woman may not prostitute herself, a Brahman may not sin, without a permit. (26)

Then he adds that whoever does wrong will be punished severely. Ghasiram started making rounds of Poona at night after eleven o'clock. He accosts anyone that he meets in the streets. He whips people. He arrests and imprisons them. The prisons are full. He harasses and punishes people on mere suspicion. He gets them tortured inhumanly when they do not confess. Revenues have increased and crimes have decreased. But the city of Poona trembles at Ghasiram's name.

Ghasiram feels satisfied with his effective persecution and now he thinks of getting his daughter married:

> I've got the Kotwali and I've got Poona straightened out! All these proud Brahmans are as soft as cotton now. No one dares to look at Ghasiram straight in the eye! Now once I find a fitting husband for my darling daughter—that piece of my heart named Lalitha Gauri—and get her married, then everything will be the way I want it. I'll make such a show of the wedding that no one's tongue will move to utter one bad word about my daughter. (37)

It is thus clear that he wants to make the marriage of his daughter a way of exercising his power. Unless he is very powerful, nobody will accept his daughter who sleeps with Nana. Gauri, the innocent lass, becomes the scapegoat of the power game. Nana enjoys sex with her and gets her killed when she becomes pregnant. Now he marries another teenage girl secretly and she will be his seventh wife. Ghasiram learns this and is heart-broken. He then murderously approaches Nana who is frightened but defiant: "Ghashya, how much more will you grieve? Now be calm. Whatever happened, protocol should not be forgotten. Don't forget that. Whom do you stand before? First you must bow. Now—bow." (43) Ghasiram like a tamed animal obeys Nana and bows but he is still angry. Nana then praises his work as the Kotwal. Then he quotes from scriptures and advises him to forget the past and to attend to his present duty:

> What has happened, happened. All the world need not know. Your good name. Your reputation is our reputation. Anyone's saying strange things about the Peshwa's Kotwal would be unbrahminical. Every care should be taken that no one anywhere speaks of this. If you hear a gossip-monger, don't wait a second longer—cut off his head! (45)

Ghasiram once sold his daughter for power and now he accepts her death only to continue exercising his power. Thus Nana cleverly stagemanages the power play and quietens Ghasiram.

Ghasiram starts acting out his fury caused by the death of Gauri. He starts murdering people. People say: "The Kotwal has acquired a penchant for human blood." They are greatly frightened. Prisons are over crowded and some die of suffocation. Poona Brahmans cannot bear it any longer. They are enraged and demand Nana to issue an order to behead Ghasiram Kotwal. Without much hesitation, Nana gives them the order and tells them to do with him whatever they like. Then he says: "Use a thorn to take out a thorn. That's great. The disease has been stopped. Anyway, there was no use for him any more." (52) The angry mob surround Ghasiram. They beat him, shave his head, paint saffron on it, ride him on a camel, tie him to the leg of an elephant and finally tie his hands behind his back. Ghasiram, overcome by remorse, says to them: "I danced on your chests but I wasted the life of my little daughter. I should be punished for the death of my daughter. Beat me. Beat me. Hit me. Cut off my hands and feet. Crack my skull." (54) The people shout around him. He succumbs to injuries and dies.

Nana, the Stage-Manager in the Game Pentagon of power, comes and addresses 'his epilogue' to the people:

> Ladies and gentlemen. Citizens of Poona. A threat to the great city of Poona has been ended today. *(The crowd cheers.)* A disease has been controlled. The demon Ghashya Kotwal, who plagued all of us, has met his death. Everything has happened according to the wishes of the gods. The mercy of the gods is with us always. (55)

He then bans the funeral rites for Ghasiram and banishes all his relatives. The people shout and cheer. Now Gulabi comes dancing. Nana's wives come dancing. All people dance happily and Nana joins them.

Nanas and Ghasirams will be there in every society as long as the hierarchies of power and the alienation that is behind them continuc to exist in our societies. The people of Poona think that Ghasiram is dead. But Ghasiram is dead only as a person while his role is very much alive and somebody will play the role. That is why Tendulkar himself aptly observes:

> Broadly speaking, I had in mind the emergence, the growth and the inevitable end of the Ghasirams; also those who create, and help Ghasirams to grow; and the irony of stoning to death a person pretending that it is the end of Ghasirams.[12]

So is the role played by the people: the Victim. They give away their power by accepting the hierarchy of power and by obeying the authorities. Tendulkar while writing the play felt the need to treat the people as a single character and so he searched for a form that suits it. He said to Samik:

> The urgency was of finding a form in which a class or a multitude could become the central character. (The present title came only

> to suggest the incident and not the character Ghasiram Kotwal.) De-glamorization of the historical incident incidentally happened because of the form and I liked it. I meant it. (viii)

Girish Karnad also explains how the form fits the theme:

> The central theatrical device in the play is the use of about a dozen singers who start conventionally enough as a chorus. But as the play progresses, they become the human curtain alternately hiding the action and revealing bits of it as in a peep show. From the neutral commentators, they slide into the role of voyeurs who enjoy the degeneration they condemn, of courtiers who perpetrate atrocities, and of the populace that suffers the harassment. (15)

The Victim resorts to voyeurism in order to enjoy the vicarious experience of power. And this prevents the people from realizing their hidden power so they perhaps play the under-dog power games.

Tendulkar's another play, *Sakharam Binder*, can also be analysed using Drama Triangle. Sakharam is actually born in a Brahmin family. His father plays the Persecutor and always beats him severely for petty reasons. Sakharam cannot bear it any longer and flees from home when he is eleven. He develops disgust for orthodox Brahminism. He gives up the Brahminical tradition and lives like a Mahar, a dirty scavenger. Thus he tries to overcome his powerlessness by rebelling against the tradition.

Sakharam rescues the women who have been victimized by the tradition. He detests the institution of marriage which is also a part of his revolt against the tradition. So, he lives with a single woman on contractual cohabitation. The woman is free to leave when she feels like leaving. Six women have left him. So, he brings Lakshmi, the seventh one, who is deserted by her husband. Sakharam thinks that he is better than any husband. He says to Lakshmi: "And you're free to take all that you've been given here. I mean clothes, *chappals*, bangles. Oh, yes. Everything good and proper, where Sakharam Binder is concerned. He's no husband to forget common decency."[13] But he proves himself to be worse than a husband. He tortures his woman if she deviates from the rules that he tyrannically imposes on her. Thus, he shifts to the role of the Persecutor, which he hates in his father. He rebels against his father and the tradition but he plays the role of his father and observes new but oppressive rules.

Lakshmi suffers a great deal yet remains compliant. She succeeds in re-Brahminizing Sakharam which results in Sakharam drinking little, swearing little, bathing regularly and praying to God. But he does not tolerate her religious obstinacy of not allowing Dawood, his Muslim friend, to join in the worship of Lord Ganesh and beats her severely. She does not yield and leaves him.

Sakharam then brings Champa, an agile woman who has deserted her sadistic husband who enjoyed inflicting pain such as putting chilly power in her genitals. She becomes frigid. She drinks liquor to overcome frigidity when Sakharam forces her to have sex. Gradually this becomes routine. He enjoys life and stops going to the press. Dawood advises him to go to the press to earn livelihood. Meanwhile, Lakshmi comes again. Sakharam does not allow her into his house. However, Champa takes pity on her and urges Sakharam to allow her. He grows impotent after Lakshmi's arrival. Champa, probably cured of frigidity, seeks sexual pleasure with Dawood. Lakshmi learns this and conveys it to him when he orders her to quit. Unable to reconcile himself to the loss of his power of sex, he strangles Champa to death in his emotion. He is shocked at what he has done. Then, Lakshmi encourages him to bury her secretly. The shift of roles is very clear: Sakharam from the Rescuer to the Persecutor; Lakshmi from the Victim to the Persecutor; and Champa from the Rescuer to the Victim. Thus, the Rescuer-Victim transaction shifts to the Persecutor-Victim transaction. This shifting of roles can also be found in Tendulkar's *Kanyadan* which is discussed in "Mental Deformity." Nath and his daughter, Jyoti, play the Rescuer while Arun, Jyoti's husband and a dalit poet, plays the Victim. Later Arun becomes the Persecutor while Jyoti and Nath become his Victims. Talking about this Jayaprakash says to Nath, his father: "In other words, yesterday's Victim is today's Victimizer."[14]

Badal Sircar's *That Other History*, like *Sakharam Binder*, exemplifies the power struggle at family level. The play is in three acts. In the first, Vasanti tells her story while in the second, Sharad, her husband narrates his story. The third is the reverie of Sharad.

Seethanath marries Kanak whose sister becomes a concubine to overcome poverty. He saves money and buys a site. He deposits some amount in a bank regularly. Kanaka is happy about it. But her drunkard father threatens him of making his wife also a concubine if he does not give him money for liquor. Seethanath yields to this blackmailing and gives him money regularly. For this, he sells the house-site and withdraws the balance of money from the bank. Thus, he allows himself to be persecuted by her father in order to rescue his wife. One day Kanaka comes to know that her husband has sold the site and also that he has drawn all the money from the bank. But he keeps the blackmailing of her father secret. She is not told the real reason, so she loses her faith in him and leaves him to follow the example of her sister. Broken-hearted, he commits suicide. Thus he persecutes himself in rescuing his wife.

In the second story, Seethanath is a teacher. He persecutes a student for reading a morbid novel *Lolita* in which Lolita, a small girl, is raped. This triggers intense guilty feelings in him as he once raped Parvati, a twelve-year beautiful girl. Now Gauri, the daughter of the headmaster, evokes erotic emotion in him. Now he is afraid of repeating the old crime with Gauri. So he sends Kanak, his wife, out and commits suicide to avert the crime. Instead of overcoming the morbid desire, he persecutes himself.

In the third, Sharad sees the other side, the negative side of history, in his reverie. He witnesses the ruthless persecution of people by cruel kings and dictators from Alexander to Hitler at various times and places from Jallianwala Bagh to Hiroshima for expanding power. Seethanath says to Sharad: "This, Sharad, is that other, the unspoken, the remaining history of thousands and thousands of years."[15] Sharad then sees Seethanath and his morbidity in himself. He feels horrified to perceive the other side of his own personality which he has never expected to exist in himself. He then wakes up from his reverie. This psychological play of Sircar throws light on the existence of the demon, the Persecutor in the personality of everybody and the havoc that it has caused throughout human history.

"Having been in a powerless position, we make ourselves feel better by taking, and assuming power over others as Rescuers or Persecutors" as Steiner rightly points out.[16] The eponymous character of Karnad's *Tughlaq* assassinates his own father and brother and becomes the king to overcome his powerlessness. He believes that he can alone rescue his people. All his reforms are exploited by the people like Aziz and thus he comes down to the role of Victim. He persecutes the people who try to obstruct his rescuing and he therefore shifts to the role of Persecutor. Soon after he returns to his original role—the Rescuer. This shifting of roles continues till the end of the play. The protagonist of Tendulkar's *Ghasiram Kotwal* is humiliated and hurt by the people of Poona. Now he is the Victim. Later he sells his own daughter to Nana and buys power by being made the Kotwal of Poona. He persecutes people ruthlessly and creates a veritable hell for them in the city. Thus he becomes the Persecutor to overcome his powerlessness. But, finally, the people take the permission of Nana and murder him after torturing and humiliating him. Thus, he ends up as a Victim. In Tendulkar's *Sakharam Binder*, Lakshmi persecutes Champa who has rescued her from Sakharam. Sircar's *That Other History* shows how everybody has in his mind the demon that is responsible for violence, destruction and wars, the other side of history.

NOTES

1. Gerald S. Blum, *Psychoanalytic Theories of Personality* (New York: McGraw, 1953) 165.
2. Interview with Augusto Boal, *Seagull Theatre Quarterly*, ed. Anjum Katyal, April 1994, 8.
3. Claude M. Steiner, *Scripts People Live* (New York: Bantam, 1980) 182.
4. Girish Karnad, *Tughlaq* (Delhi: Oxford UP, 1987) 1.
5. Girish Karanad, 'Interview,' *Enact*, June 1971, no page.
6. Aparna Dharwadker, "Historical Fictions and Postcolonial Representation: Reading Girish Karnad's *Tughlaq*," *PMLA*, Vol. 110, No. 1, Jan. 1995, 47.
7. Sukrat and Aflatoon refer to Socrates and Plato.
8. Veena Noble Dass, *Modern India Drama in English Translation* (New Delhi, 1988) 147.
9. Qtd. Samik Bandyopadhyay, 'Introduction,' *Ghasiram Kotwal* by Vijay Tendulkar, trans. Jayant Karve & Eleanor Zelliot. (Calcutta: Seagull Books, 1986) iv.
10. 'Author's Introduction,' *Three Plays* (Delhi: Oxford UP, 1994) 15.
11. *Transactional Game Analysis* (Delhi: Manohar, 1979) 153.
12. Qtd. Samik Bandyopadhyaya, v.
13. Vijay Tendulkar, *Sakharam Binder*, trans. Kumud Mehta & Shanta Gokhale, *Five Plays* (Bombay: Oxford UP, 1992) 135.
14. Vijay Tendulkar, *Kanyadan*, trans. Gowri Ramnarayan (Delhi: Oxford UP, 1996) 51.
15. Baḍal Sircar, *That Other History*, trans. Vinod L. Doshi, *Enact*, Sept.-Oct. 1980, 22.
16. Steiner, 182.

Physical Deformity: Karnad's *Hayavadana*, Tendulkar' *Sakharam Binder* and Sircar's *Evam Indrajit*

> Your body bathed in a river, swam and danced in it. Shouldn't your head know what river it was, what swim? Your head too must submerge in that river—the flow must rumple your hair, run its tongue in your ears and press your head to its bosom. Until that's done, you'll continue to be incomplete.
>
> *Hayavadana*

Gender and social deformities invade the human body too and cause physical deformity. Gender and social hierarchies are translated psychosomatically in individual human beings. People accept the cultural attributes of their roles as men and women and as workers and intellectuals. Therefore the attributes determine their life styles to the extent that they are internalized. These life styles, like genes, shape their bodies and cause deformities within the biological boundaries. As Brahmins (intellectuals) are considered superior to Shudras (workers) in a society, the brain (head) is considered superior to the body in an individual. Therefore, "Some people even feel that their bodies are a lesser part of them, even that they are cursed by having a body" as rightly observed by Steiner.[1]

Brahmins are mentally brilliant but physically weak as they spend most of their time in reading and writing. Shudras are mentally dull but physically strong as they spend most of their time in manual work. And women are physically weak and mentally dull as they, being confined to housework, are not allowed to exercise their mind and body very hard. Even among workers, those parts of their bodies that are used more in their occupation become stronger than other parts. For example, a cyclerickshaw driver gets strong legs while a blacksmith gets strong arms. Adept, strong right hands and inept, weak left hands are a striking evidence of physical deformity caused by cultural attributes all over the world.

Physical deformity reflects not only gender and social deformities but also political deformity. The head is more powerful than the body. So, within an individual, the head governs the body, whether the individual is a man, a woman, an intellectual or a worker. It is the head that carries the cultural attributes and thus it is the head that determines the life style of the individual. The head usually undermines the wisdom of the body and thus causes joylessness, drug addiction and ill health.

Actually the body and the mind were once in an undifferentiated unity which we have lost in course of civilization. Most of the people do not even know that they can be unified. Gayelord Hauser says: "You know that mind and body are one, that mind and body and emotion are one. You know that the body can affect the mind just as the mind can affect the body. You will not treat yourself as two different persons."[2] This is what William Blake describes as 'the undivided body-soul.'[3] According to Norman O. Brown,[4] a psychoanalyst, primitive human beings enjoyed perfect harmony between their mind and body; their mind felt their bodily experiences and their body rocked with the feelings of their mind. Brown calls this undifferentiated and unified body and mind the *Dionysian ego*. In the process of civilization, he argues, the mind and the body are divided, differentiated and alienated from each other. Because of the split and alienation between them, the experiences of the body do not reach the mind and the feelings of the mind do not spread through the body. Steiner attributes joylessness to this. (169) Brown calls the differentiated and alienated mind and body the *Apollonian ego*. Hauser also perceives this evil effect of civilization: "That turn in civilization that has increased cerebral activity and decreased manual functions leaves the mind unhappy and the hand itching for something to do." (104-5) The disharmony of the mind and the body reflects that of Brahmins and Shudras.

The alienation and antagonism between the mind and the body inevitably leads to physical deformity, joylessness and ill health. People become addicted to alcohol, drugs and useless consumerism to escape from joylessness and to feel elated. Alcohol and drugs offer only a fleeting experience of elation but spoil health severely and augment the alienation. Steiner explains how joylessness is exploited: "Joylessness is unfortunately exploited by business interests. Drug use and consumerism are widely encouraged through the media and large number of people's lives depend upon the expenditures of a joyless population on drugs and essentially useless consumer items." (168) Sometimes the idealism, infused through education and mass media into the mind of the people, serves the purpose of drug addiction. It provides them illusory pleasure of realizing their ideal but finally leads to their disillusionment and disappointment. The alienation of the mind and the body impairs our perception also. As Steiner observes, "Children's eidetic vision is turned into impoverished perception of grownups." (168) He argues that people go for violence, sexual excess and drug abuse as they ignore the wisdom of their bodies. (168) All these aspects of physical deformity find expression in Karnad's *Hayavadana*, Tendulkar's *Sakharam Binder* and Sircar's *Evam Indrajit*.

The theme of *Hayavadana*[5] is the problem of physical deformity caused by the alienation of the mind (head) and the body. This is suggested by the reference to 'incompleteness' and 'completeness.' For instance, Kapila questions: "Why should one tolerate this mad dance of incompleteness?"[6] and the Bhagavata blesses Hayavadana: "May you become successful in your search for completeness." (11) The play starts with the worship and then the description of Lord Ganesha, the elephant-headed god, who symbolises physical deformity. This hints at the theme. The Bhagavata says: "An elephant's head on a human body, a broken tusk and a cracked belly—whichever way you look at him he seems the embodiment of imperfection, of incompleteness. How indeed can one fathom the mystery that this very Vakratunda-Mahakaya, with his crooked face and distorted body, is the Lord of Success and Perfection?" (1) As the Bhagavata introduces the story and the characters of the main plot, Hayavadana, the eponymous character comes onto the stage. Like Ganesha, Hayavadana the horse-headed man, also suggests physical deformity. The Bhagavata mistakes his head for the mask and tries to pull it off with the help of an actor but fails. Then he learns from Hayavadana that he is born with a horse head as his mother married a stallion, a cursed Gandharva. Hayavadana has been striving to become complete through various religious penances and social service for several years. On the advice of the Bhagavata, he goes to Goddess Kali to seek her blessings.

The play proper begins now. Devadatta is a Brahmin. He reads and writes. He develops his mind and ignores his body. He writes excellent poetry and defeats several scholars in discussions. Kapila is a blacksmith. He plays games and participates in sports. He defeats many wrestlers in competitions. He has manual skills and is adept in making and mending carts and other things. He develops his body and neglects his mind. While describing their friendship, the Bhagavata says: 'One mind, one heart.' Devadatta is 'the mind' and Kapila is 'the heart.' Actually their friendship is based on the fact that they depend on each other for what each lacks. That is why Raykar points out: "They are thus complementary to each other."[7] Since the mind is considered superior to the body in our society, the caste of Brahmins occupies the highest rung in the Hindu society which is hierarchized caste-wise. That is why Devadatta sits on a chair while Kapila squats on the floor. Their friendship is only superficial, not real, as real love is not possible between unequal people.

Devadatta is 'the mind' and Kapila, 'the body.' And both suffer from the alienation of the mind and the body. Devadatta easily perceives his feelings of love as his mind is nimble but he lacks the initiative as his body is passive. So, he falls in love fifteen times in a period of two years. Yet he fails to marry any of the girls. Kapila cannot perceive the bodily sensations of love as his mind is not nimble but he has the initiative and arranges things easily as his body is agile. Devadatta knows this. So he seeks his help when even his sixteenth love affair seems to be a fiasco. He expresses his utter helplessness and hopelessness: "I swear, Kapila, with you as my witness, if I ever get her as my wife, I'll sacrifice my two arms to the goddess Kali, I'll sacrifice my head to Lord Rudra." (14) Kapila easily arranges his marriage with Padmini. He takes Devadatta and his wife in a cart on a trip. Padmini appreciates his dexterity in driving the cart and later his strong handsome body. Devadatta feels agonized to see Padmini gaze at Kapila with love. So, he goes to the temple of Kali and beheads himself when Padmini and Kapila visit the temple of Rudra. Later, Kapila goes in search of Devadatta and finds him dead at the temple of Kali. He expresses his wish to follow his friend and beheads himself. Actually, he becomes aware of the vague sensation of his infatuation; an obscure fear of being blamed for the death of Devadatta and for his infatuation for Padmini seizes him. But he does not admit it. Kali uncovers the hypocrisy of the friends when she prevents Padmini from committing harakiri. She says: "They were lying to their last breaths." (33) She grants Padmini's wish to revive them. In her haste, Padmini transposes their heads. Devadatta and Kapila are revived with their heads transposed.[8]

The person with Devadatta's head and Kapila's body is called Devadatta and the other person with Kapila's head and Devadatta's body is called Kapila in the play. Each claims Padmini as his wife.

KAPILA. This is the hand that accepted her at the wedding. This the body she's lived with all these months. And the child she's carrying is the seed of this body. (36-37)

DEVADATTA. Of all the human limbs the topmost—in position as well as in importance—is the head. I have

Devadatta's head and it follows that I am Devadatta. (37)

In this argument Padmini favours and supports Devadatta. Kapila then discloses her intention: "I know what you want, Padmini. Devadatta's clever head and Kapila's strong body." (38) Finally, they seek the advice of a *rishi* (saint). The *rishi* says that the person with Devadatta's head is the rightful husband of Padmini since the head is the supreme of all the parts of the body. Kapila feels utterly disappointed and dejected. Devadatta and Padmini return to Dharmapura, their hometown very happily and plunge into the joys of married life. Padmini does not understand the power of the head. So, she also mistakes juxtaposition of the head and the body for their unification. So, she feels elated to live with Devadatta's new body. She does not foresee that her joy is short-lived. The Brahminical hypothesis that the head is the supreme organ in the body reflects the social hierarchy in which the caste of Brahmins is supreme in the society.

Devadatta goes to the gymnasium and participates in sports. He even defeats a wrestler who challenges the people to fight with him. Padmini is happy about his physical prowess but warns him not to outdo lest his acquisition of Kapila's body should be discovered. The two dolls that he brought from Ujjain for his son talk about his vigour.

DOLL II. with his rough labourer's hands.
DOLL I. Palms like wood. . .
DOLL II. A grip like a vice . . . (44)

Devadatta resumes his Brahminical life style and gradually loses the physical vigour of Kapila's body. Padmini asks him why he does not go out. He replies that he has to observe his duty as a Brahmin and then he adds: "It was fun the first few days because it was new. All that muscle and strength. But how long can one go on like that? I have the family tradition to maintain—the daily reading, writing and studies." (46) The Dolls also talk about this change of his body:

DOLL I. His palms! They were so rough, when he first brought us here. Like a labourer's. But now they are soft—sickly soft—like a young girl's.
DOLL II. I know, I've noticed something too.
DOLL I. What?
DOLL II. His stomach. It was so tight and muscular. Now . . .

DOLL I. I know. It's loose . . .
DOLL II. Do you think it'll swell up too? (47)

Similarly Kapila's head carries the attributes of a craftsman and athlete. He does hard work and regains his physical vigour. Thus he gradually loses the softness and weakness of Devadatta's body. Padmini loses interest in Devadatta on account of his weak soft body with a pot belly. Her unconscious mind longs for Kapila. She sees Kapila vaguely in her dreams and the Dolls talk about it. She asks Devadatta to throw out the old dolls and bring new ones for their son from Ujjain. Doll II says; "Cover your wife before you start worrying about our rags." (52) When Devadatta leaves for Ujjain, Padmini takes her son and goes into the forest. She meets Kapila who realizes the power of the head. Unable to reconcile herself to this reality, she asks Kapila a tragic rhetorical question, "Must the head always win?" and he answers: "That's why I am Kapila now." (56) She knows that Devadatta became completely Devadatta because the head won. Actually, it is the victory of the cultural hegemony that has shaped the minds of Devadatta and Kapila. But Padmini still says: "Yes, you won Kapila. Devadatta won too. But I the better half of two bodies—I neither win nor lose." (57) In fact, the names and the personalities of Devadatta and Kapila are the products of the culture which is based on the deformities. It is their bodies, representing life or Nature, that have lost the battle.

The conflict of the mind and the body is more acute in Kapila than in Devadatta. Devadatta, after discontinuing his physical exercise, often feels like going to the gymnasium. He gets bodily pains and decides not to do any physical exercise anymore. Thus, he overcomes the memories of Kapila's body. But Kapila really has a very hard task to overcome the erotic memories of Devadatta's body though he succeeds in making the body strong through physical exercises. So he says:

> One beats the body into shape, but one can't beat away the memories in it. Isn't that surprising? That the body should have its own ghosts—its own memories? Memories of touch—memories of a touch—memories of a body swaying in these arms, of a warm skin against this palm—memories which one cannot recognize, cannot understand, cannot even name because this head wasn't there when they happened. (57-58)

He asks Padmini why she has come and why she has touched him. He then adds: "I have never touched you, but this body, this appendage laughed and flowered out in a festival of memories to which I'm an outcaste." (58) Padmini intuitively feels that the conflict is due to alienation. She chides him for his stupidity and says: "Your body bathed in a river, swam and danced in it. Shouldn't your head know what river it was, what swim? Your head too must submerge in that river—the flow must rumple your hair, run its tongue in your ears and press your head to its bosom. Until that's done, you'll continue to be incomplete." (58) She means that the reunification of the mind and the body is the only solution of their physical deformity and its ill effects.

Kapila asks Padmini to go to Devadatta but she requests him to allow her to stay there and look at him for a while. Later, Devadatta comes and asks Kapila whether he also loves Padmini. Kapila answers him affirmatively and suggests that they live like the five Pandavas and Draupadi of the *Mahabharata.* As Padmini does not consent to this, they fight a duel and kill each other. Thus they end their 'mad dance of incompleteness.' Padmini still wants to achieve the unification of the mind and the body through her son. So she wants to provide her son both physical and mental training. She therefore relates her will to the Bhagavata:

> My son is sleeping in the hut. Take him under your care. Give him to the hunters who live in the forests and tell them it's Kapila's son. They loved Kapila and will bring the child up. Let the child grow up in the forest with the rivers and the trees. When he's five take him to the Revered Brahmin Vidyasagara of Dharmapura. Tell him it's Devadatta's son. (62)

Then she commits *sati* and thus ends her failure in unifying the mind and the body.

Padmini's son grows among the hunters in the forest for five years according to her oral will and is then sent to the Bhagavata. The boy is as morose as Kapila in the forest. He does not play and does not laugh as a child should do. They try to make him laugh but fail. Meanwhile Hayavadana comes and he is a complete horse now. He says that Goddess Kali has granted his wish to be complete. What he regrets is the retention of human voice. He tries to break his human voice by singing various patriotic songs but in vain. Padmini's son sees Hayavadana, a horse, speak and laugh. He sheds his gloom and starts laughing and then clapping his hands and the dolls fall out of his hands. Then he accepts the request of Hayavadana to sing a song and Hayavadana gives him a ride while he sings a song. The boy then asks him to laugh. As Hayavadana tries to laugh, his laughter ends up as a proper neigh and thus he loses his human voice. Hayavadana and Padmini's son become complete as if they were freed from the spell by each other. Both are very happy and the boy enjoys riding the horse. Then the Bhagavata says: "So at long last Hayavadana has become complete. (*To the Actors.*) You two go and tell the Revered Brahmin Vidyasagara that his grandson is returning home in triumph, riding a big, white charger." (71) The boy riding the horse symbolizes the reunification of man and Nature. Thus, Padmini succeeds in achieving her goal posthumously.

Most of the critics, including M.K. Naik and Shubhangi S. Raykar, argue that it is humanly impossible to achieve perfection. Of course, it is impossible to achieve perfection as long as physical deformity is sustained by cultural hegemony. A. Jaganmohanachary rightly points out that Devadatta loses his physical vigour only because he discontinues the physical exercise in order to pursue his Brahminical tradition. But Raykar in her brilliant paper on *Hayavadana* argues that the unification of Apollo and Dionysus symbolized by Devadatta and Kapila respectively is not at all possible. Brown uses the words, Apollo and Dionysus, to represent alienation and unification respectively. Following the model of Brown, it can be concluded that the play deals with the three phases of human history and Karnad is successful in this as he cleverly exploits Indian myth and folk theatre (Yakshagana bayalata of Karnataka). Hayavadana and his mother who is cursed to become a mare by her husband stand for the first phase when primitive human beings like animals enjoyed Dionysian ego: the undifferentiated and unified body-mind. Hayavadana's father, a handsome stallion, becomes a celestial man, *Gandharva*. This symbolizes the process of human civilization when man attains Apollonian ego by losing Dionysian ego gradually. So Devadatta and Kapila who represent the modern man suffer from the problems caused by their Apollonian egos. As they cannot get rid of their Apollonian egos, they end their lives. Veena Noble Dass observes: "In Devadatta Karnad does not show the superiority of the mind, rather he shows its limitations."[9] These limitations are the result of the hegemony of Apollonian culture where the mind and the body become differentiated, alienated and antagonistic. Kapila and Devadatta are both victims of this and their predicament is that of the modern man. The third phase of human history emerges when the mind and the body are reunified in an undifferentiated unity. Padmini's son will stand for the future man who will be able to achieve this. This concept of alienation and physical deformity easily answers the two riddles of the play: why does Hayavadana's mother feel happy when her husband curses her to become a mare and why does Goddess Kali make Hayavadana a complete horse instead of a complete man? This is because animals have no alienation and no deformity.

Sakharam Binder is probably Tendulkar's most intensely naturalistic play as Arundhati Banerjee puts it in her introduction to *Five Plays* of Tendulkar.[10] The play ignores the cultural norms and boldly presents the crude perversions caused by physical deformity. The three major characters, Sakharam, Lakshmi and Champa, are all abnormal and each is unique in his or her abnormality. Sakharam speaks vulgar language, drinks liquor, smokes and indulges in mechanical sex; Lakshmi is obstinately conventional and her religiosity amounts to unrealistic and inhuman fundamentalism. And Champa is as rebellious as Sakharam and does almost all the things that he does. They do whatever they do, in order to overcome the alienation and the joylessness that they suffer. Paradoxically, their actions effect the illusion of joy that sustains joylessness. And their discontent in life betrays this.

Sakharam is treated negatively by his own parents and the feelings of his tender heart are hurt deeply. He says to Lakshmi: "Born naked, I was. My mother used to say, the brat's shameless. He's *Mahar* born in a Brahmin home. And if I was, who's to blame? It wasn't my doing."[11] Then he tells her how his father made him run away from home.

> Born in a *Brahmin* family, but I'm a *Mahar*, a dirty scavenger. I call that a bloody joke! I ran away from home when I was eleven. Got fed up with my father's beatings. Nothing I did ever seemed right. You'd think I was his enemy or something. The way he'd thrash me! (127)

The cruel, prejudiced treatment of Sakharam by his parents has caused him to behave rebelliously in order to overcome his powerlessness and joylessness. Though he hates his father, he follows him in many ways. He is as bad-tempered as he. He lets himself be Brahminized a little by Lakshmi. He worships God regularly. Though he denounces the conventional marriage, husbands and wives, he not only behaves like any husband but also sympathizes with him. At one time, he says to Lakshmi: "You get kicked by your husbands and you go and fall at their feet," (135) and at another, he objects to Champa's ill-treatment of her morbid husband: "What kind of a woman are you? Look, what you've done to him! He's your husband. Haven't you a heart?" (167) He laughs at the loyalty of women to their inhuman husbands yet he demands complete loyalty to him from his women. "If it's a stranger, you'll have to cover your head and answer him. If I'm not at home, don't admit anyone." (156) He strangles Champa when he learns that she is not loyal to him. He lives with only one woman at a time though on a contractual cohabitation. It is as good as a formal marriage. He is not less cruel than his father. Lakshmi says to him:

> I've never heard a kind word here. Always barking orders. Curses. Oaths. Threatening to throw me out. Kicks and blows. . . . There I was in agony after I'd been belted, and all you wanted me to do was laugh. Laugh and laugh again. Here I am on the point of death and I'm supposed to laugh. Hell must be a better place than this. . . . If I die, I'll be free of this once and for all. (148)

He is able to be so cruel only because of his self-alienation, the split between his mind and body which must have been caused by the thrashing of his father. He internally feels powerless and joyless. He uses rough language; he smokes tobacco and opium; he drinks liquor and enjoys mechanical sex in order to overcome this. He forces Lakshmi to laugh to stimulate him sexually though she suffers from a severe burn on her foot. When Lakshmi leaves him, he brings Champa and forces her to give him sexual pleasure. He does not bother about the pain and the pleasure of his partner in this. All these activities provide him mythical joy and he feels complacent about himself and his life. Only Champa disturbs his complacency.

Lakshmi is deserted by her husband because she does not beget any children. She seeks shelter under the roof of Sakharam. She is not a Brahmin; yet she observes Brahminical culture. She tries to overcome her powerlessness and joylessness in doing so. She proves to be obedient and loyal to her man; yet she bravely objects to his unbrahminical ways. Sakharam slaps her hard for not allowing Dawood, his friend to join the prayer to Lord Ganapati; yet she says: "What's wrong with what I said? How can a Muslim join in a prayer to *Ganapati*?" (144) Neither Sakharam nor Lakshmi compromises on this. And it results in her leaving him. This shows her fundamentalism. Sakharam proves to be more humane in this than Lakshmi. She talks to an ant, laughs and plays with it. But she fails to communicate with human beings properly. Sakharam demands her to laugh with him as spontaneously as she does with the ant. After leaving Sakharam, she goes to her nephew for shelter. He and his wife accuse her of stealing to get rid of her. As she has no alternative, she returns to Sakharam. But Sakharam beats her and urges her to get out. However, Champa comes to her rescue and she is allowed to live with them. So, Lakshmi does the housework and worships her gods. She nurses Champa's husband and denounces her for ill-treating him. She is disgusted to learn that Champa flirts with Dawood. She tells Sakharam about Champa's disloyalty.

He strangles Champa to death and feels aghast at his own action. She advises him to bury her secretly in the house itself.

> Anyway she was a sinner. She'll go to hell. Not you. I've been a virtuous woman. My virtuous deeds will see both of us through. I'll stay with you. I'll look after you. I'll do what you say. And I'll die with my head on your lap. Yes. Now don't be afraid. We'll—we'll bury her. Where do you think? Not out there—no. Somewhere here. Inside. And we'll say that she went away. No one will suspect. I'll swear by God. He knows everything. He knows I am virtuous. He'll stand by me. He won't judge you. I'll tell him to count my good deeds as yours. I'll do everything for you. (196-97)

Thus, she goes to any extent even inhumanly to effect what she believes to be right. She prefers tradition to human beings. So, she accepts a husband however cruel he may be and she detests Champa for her disloyalty though the latter rescues her from Sakharam. She also envies Champa for her sway over Sakharam. Above all, she believes that the patriarchal tradition which has been in vogue for ages is right and sacred though it has caused immense suffering to all the women since its emergence. Because of the alienation of the mind and the body, she does not understand the inhuman and harmful nature of the tradition. As she observes it, she finds in it some power and joy which are merely mythical and her powerlessness and joylessness continue. Her unsympathetic persecution of Champa is, in a way, due to her self-alienation.

Champa is the antithesis of Lakshmi. She never bothers about the tradition. She is confident and courageous. Her mother sells liquor and tobacco. Fouzdar Shinde comes to the shop on a raid and sees Champa. He takes her away from her mother even before she becomes a woman. He tortures her by branding her, sticking needles into her and making her do awful things. So, she is terribly frightened and runs away. He brings her back and puts chilly powder in her genitals. All this causes self-alienation in her too and makes her frigid. So, she detests sex. As she grows bold, she leaves Shinde and joins Sakharam. She first resists his attempts to have sex with her. But, later, she yields to him as she sees no better alternative: "Face half a dozen animals every day! Easier to put up with this one." (181) But she drinks liquor before she goes to bed with him.

> CHAMPA. You'll have your fun . . . . Wait. I'll give it to you. [*Keeps on drinking and making him drink. Laughs*

uncontrollably.] Fun for anyone who comes along. A dog. A corpse even. (171)

The compulsive sex of Sakharam exhausts her completely and she complains: "My head and body—just a bundle of pains and aches." (179) Later, she says to Lakshmi: "But your Sakharam, he really takes his money's worth out of a woman." (181) She has little faith in religion and tells Lakshmi the reality of life: "They don't come and live your hell for you—those gods and Brahmins." (180) Her language is as vulgar as that of Sakharam who says: "In this house the woman must always speak with restraint. I won't put up with bad language." (158) Somehow Sakharam grows impotent after the arrival of Lakshmi. Now, Champa objects to Sakharam's approach to her: "I didn't mind it as long as you were a man. I won't take you now?" (193) She likes Dawood, Sakharam's friend when he arrives. She expresses this repeatedly: "He is nice" (159-60) and evokes envy in Sakharam who says: "But in this house, I won't allow too much talking to strangers." (160) She appreciates the tea made by Dawood and the nice pan with tobacco brought by him. Finally, she enjoys sex with Dawood when Sakharam becomes impotent. She finds human love more in Dawood than in Sakharam. She is honest in what she does. Unlike Lakshmi, she prefers human goodness to inhuman tradition and unlike Sakharam, she breaks the tradition in order to be human and humane. But she cannot forgive her husband because he has torn her heart. (167) Shinde and Sakharam have tormented her. She takes tobacco and liquor to numb the sensations of pain in her body. Thus, she also suffers from self alienation—the alienation of the mind and the body. However, she does not suffer from powerlessness as Sakharam and Lakshmi do.

Veena Noble Dass applies the concepts of psychoanalysis to analyse *Sakhram Binder*. She observes: "It was in essence a protest against exorbitant demands of society, especially in the sexual sphere, on the life of the individual."(103) Renuka calls Sakharam 'a dehumanised brutal wretch.'[12] But, it is to be understood that he like any other character is a product of our dehumanizing culture. Tendulkar says: "Even in plays like *Sakharam Binder* and *The Vultures*, the theme is not violence. Violence comes as a way of life—a natural way of life if you consider the background of the characters. It is there as part of the functioning of a character."[13] The inhuman violence of the human characters in these plays is only the result of the physical deformity. Ramakant, Umakant and Manik drink liquor and resort to violence, in Tendulkar's *Vultures*, to overcome their deep-rooted joylessness. Alienation corrupts and perverts all human values, as Marx puts it.

Evam Indrajit by Badal Sircar deals with a new aspect of physical deformity through the eponymous character. Amal, Vimal and Kamal form the background for this. They take the routine life for granted and try to overcome their joylessness by being busy doing the things that their civilized life demands. But, Indrajit, like the mythical character, the son of Ravana who defeats Indra the Hindu Zeus, is a rebel. He is conscious of and bored with routine, mundane life. He, therefore, cannot find any joy in it and wants to be different in order to overcome his joylessness. In his endeavour to be different, he goes round and finally reaches the point where he starts. So, he realizes that he cannot escape from the routine. He admits that he is Nirmal, one of them, but not Indrajit. At last he thinks, "Dying! That is the greatest happiness."[14]

As the play starts, Writer searches for a theme to write a play but finds none. Manasi advises him to write about four middle-class people who come late. So he invites them onto the stage. He asks for their names. They are Amal, Vimal, Kamal and Indrajit. Writer then describes them:

> According to the census of 1961, the population of Calcutta is 2,92,12,891. Of them about two and a half per cent are graduates. They are known by different names. They are the middle-income group, although within that group there is enough disparity of income. They are the intellectuals, although if they really relied on their intellect, they would die of starvation. They are educated minority, if a degree is indeed a mark of education. They are the elite, because they are well aware of their difference from the rest. They are Amal, Vimal, Kamal . . . And Indrajit. (5-6)

Auntie then asks him to have his meal. Manasi asks him whether he has written anything. He answers in the negative. Then, he regrets his ignorance of the toil and suffering of peasants and workers. It is, thus, shown that writer is also one of them, the elite and the middle-income group.

The three acts of the play portray the three major phases of the lives of Amal, Vimal and Kamal. The first Act dramatizes their studies, examinations, hobbies, pastimes and other things that characterize their college life. They get jobs and marry in the second Act. They have various ambitions in their life and achieve them in the third: Amal gets a promotion as a manager in ABC Company; Vimal buys a plot and builds a house there; and Kamal starts business to earn more money. Indrajit loves Manasi, his first cousin on his mother's side and wants to marry her which is a taboo. And he wants to visit London and this visit, he believes, will liberate him from the banality of life. His awareness of the ennui of life which Amal, Vimal and Kamal lack makes him rebellious and restless. He says, in a proud manner, to Manasi: "If I hadn't tasted the fruit of knowledge I could have gone on living this paradise of your blessed society of rules. Now I can only batter my head against the wall." (23) He changes his job from Calcutta to Bhopal. Then he gets a transferable job and goes to Bombay, Jullunder, Meerut and Udaypur. Manasi does not agree to marry him against the taboo and becomes a school teacher in Calcutta. She and he write letters to each other and meet once a year in Calcutta. He visits London but this does not change his life in any way. Then, he marries another Manasi and leads marital life. He tells Manasi about his family: "My wife looks after the house. I work in the office. My wife goes to a film. I go with her. My wife goes to her parents' house. I eat in a restaurant. She comes back. I go marketing." (54) Thus, he falls into the whirlpool of banal life that he has striven hard to shun. He realizes at last that he is not different from others. He talks about his disillusionment:

> INDRAJIT. so long as I couldn't accept my ordinariness I dreamt. Now I accept it.
> MANASI. Indrajit . . .
> INDRAJIT. No, Manasi, don't call me Indrajit, please don't. I am Nirmal. Amal, Vimal, Kamal and Nirmal. Amal, Vimal, Kamal and Nirmal . . . (58 59)

When he sees no sense in living, Writer enlightens him on existential philosophy:

> Walk! Be on the road! For us there is only the road. We shall walk. I know nothing to write about—still I shall have to write. You have nothing to say—still you will have to talk. Manasi has nothing to live for—she will have to live. For us there is only the road—so walk on. We are the cursed spirits of Sisyphus. We have to push the rock to the top—even if it just rolls down. (59)

It is the theme. The playwright thus conveys the philosophy of existentialism to the elite of the middle-income group who feel too frustrated with banal life to live on.

K.Venkata Reddy, Veena Noble Dass and Eakambaram agree that *Evam Indrajit* is an absurd play. Eakambaram calls it an Indian version of *Waiting for Godot*. He strongly feels that the play is not relevant to Indian context. He believes Indians do not suffer from alienation because,

"We may be poor and downtrodden, but the qualities of patience, endurance, hope, and peace which Hinduism and other religions embody enable us to survive."[15] But alienation is an indispensable part and process of civilization whatever the civilization may be. And in India, the higher castes of the Hinduism practise the inhuman convention of untouchability as alienation dehumanizes people. The physical deformity that people acquire through being civilized alienates them from the very source of life and they feel life to be meaningless. Indrajit's predicament arises out of his awareness which is alienated from his bodily wisdom. Writer also faces the same plight. Veena Noble Dass observes: "His agony is the agony of the artist who is deeply aware of the sterility and horror that is life." (47) Satyadev Dubey, commenting on the elite of India in general and those of Bengal in particular, points out:

> The intellectually alive urban middle class regards itself as the backbone of the country. Their so-called middle class values have been glorified and yet their genuine and deeper values have always been attacked by fashionable Marxist dogmas. The middle classes have been made to feel guilty for opting for stability, aspiring for culture and believing in a national identity. In Bengal, the contradiction was resolved at a certain level with the middle classes aligning themselves with the left forces. (Introduction, ii)

Sircar's *There's No End* is like his *Evam Indrajit*. The protagonist of the play, Sumanta, a Bengali young intellectual like Indrajit, faces the same problem. Sumanta is more progressive than Indrajit. He loves Manika when he is a student but he does not marry her. Then, he discontinues his studies and plunges into the struggle organised by Communist Party. The railway strike of 1949 fails and he becomes disillusioned and leaves Communist Party. Then, he resumes his studies and completes M.Sc. Instead of doing research in Chemistry, he joins as a Research Assistant in S.K. Industries and becomes a Junior Executive on promotion. He dislikes the duties of the post and loses the job by deliberately committing a mistake. He and Sumati become friends. Presently, he is a writer of good reputation. One day, he is arrested and taken to court. His mother, his lover, his leader of the Party, his professor and his employer accuse him of betraying them. Five more witnesses find fault with his not writing about the poor people, workers and the victims of communal riots and world wars. Sumanta's disillusionment with the Communist movement reflects that of Sircar himself though he favours the leftist: "The discovery that some respected leaders were liars and cheats who duped their followers led to disillusionment."[16] The trial finally proves that every human being is a culprit. All human beings have brought about this crisis and all of them suffer in one way or another. Therefore, they all can resolve it collectively.

SUMANTA. There is no accused. I am the accused. You . . . you . . . all of you are accused. We are all the accused.
THE MAN. We are all the accused.
THE JURY. (*together*) We are all the accused.[17]

The play thus shows that we can overcome alienation only through unification characterized by collective awareness and endeavour.

Mohan Rakesh's short play, *Perhaps*, illustrates how physical deformity can lead to mental deformity. It is a dialogue between a man and his wife about the problems of their life. Like Indrajit, they also feel bored with the banality of their routine life. The repetition deprives them of their joy. They feel dejected:

MAN.	Don't you feel that the things we used to enjoy at one time . . . no longer bring us happiness?
WOMAN.	I've decided.
MAN.	What?
WOMAN.	That things will always remain the same and we'll have to go on like this for years. (*sobs*)
MAN.	Everything repeats itself. When we have already lived we shall have to live again . . .[18]

They face the same predicament as Indrajit does. The man summarizes their problems "one can do what one likes but the emptiness within one still remains . . ." (11) The mind has nothing meaningful once it is alienated from the body. It feels empty and it may go mad. The man admits: "I don't get upset. . . . I'm made to get upset." (10)

Division and hierarchization invade the human body. The mind and the body are divided and the mind is considered superior to the body. The mind carries the cultural deformity in itself and governs the body. It suppresses the spontaneity of the body and causes physical deformity. This finds a comprehensive elucidation in Karnad's *Hayavadana*. Devadatta, as a Brahmin, has a brilliant mind and a weak body whereas Kapila, as a Shudra, has a strong body and a dull mind. Padmini, Devadatta's wife, juxtaposes their heads at the temple of Goddess Kali. So Devadatta gets Kapila's strong body and Kapila gets Devadatta's weak body. But finally, the head wins—Devadatta discontinues physical exercise and gets back his weak body while Kapila toils in the forest and becomes strong again. The eponymous character becomes a complete horse instead of a complete man as Goddess Kali grants his wish to be complete. Hayavadana's mother runs away happily when his father curses her to become a mare. This shows that animals unlike human beings are free from physical deformity caused by culture. The alienation between the mind and the body, the major cause of physical deformity, makes people joyless and their life meaningless as the bodily sensations are suppressed and prevented from reaching the mind. So people seek to get pleasure by consuming alcohol and drugs and by indulging in mechanical sex and violence. In Tendulkar's *Sakharam Binder*, the protagonist and Champa drink liquor and enjoy loveless sex whereas Lakshmi tries to drown her joylessness in religious rituals. In Sircar's *Evam Indrajit*, the eponymous character vainly strives to make his life meaningful and joyful by being different from common folk. In his play, *There's No End*, the central character goes on changing his course of life for the same purpose.

NOTES

1. Claude M. Steiner, *Scripts People Live* (New York: Bantam, 1980) 168.
2. *Be Happier Be Healthier* (New York: Popular Library, 1954) 162.
3. Qtd. Richard Ellmann and Charles Feidelson Jr., *The Modern Tradition* (New York: Oxford UP, 1965) 539.
4. "Apollo and Dionysus," *Life Against Death*, (London: Routledge, 1959) 155-76.
5. The story of Hayavadana resembles that of Hayahaya who is the son of Goddess Lakshmi, cursed by Lord Vishnu to become a mare because she gazes at the handsome stallion of Revata.
6. Girish Karnad, *Hayavadana* (New Delhi: Oxford UP, 1988) 40.
7. Shubhangi S. Raykar, "The Development of Girish Karnad as a Dramatist: *Hayavadana*," *The Studies in Contemporary Indian Drama*, ed. Sudhakar Pandey & Freya Taraporewala (New Delhi: Prestige, 1990) 50.
8. Karnad borrows this from Thomas Mann's *The Transposed Heads* which is a modified and elaborated version of the sixth story of *Vetala panchavimsati*.
9. Veena Noble Dass, *Modern Indian Drama in English Translation* (New Delhi: np, 1988) 158.
10. Arundhati Banerjee, 'Introduction,' *Five Plays*, Vijay Tendulkar (Bombay: Oxford UP, 1992) xiii.
11. Vijay Tendulkar, *Sakharam Binder*, trans. Kumud Mehta & Shanta Gokhale, *Five Plays* (Bombay: Oxford UP, 1992) 127.

12. E. Renuka, All about Umbugland: A Study of Vijay Tendulkar's Plays, diss, Kakatiya University, 1984, 138.
13. Vijay Tendulkar, 'Interview,' *The Indian Express*, March 27, 1983, Magazine Section, 5.
14. Badal Sircar, *Evam Indrajit*, trans. Girish Karnad (Calcutta: Oxford UP, 1974), 49.
15. N. Eakambaram, "Validity of *Evam Indrajit*—An Indian Version of an Absurb Play," *Essays in Criticism on Indian Literature in English*, ed. M.S. Nagarajan et. al. (New Delhi: S. Chand, 1991) 15 and 21.
16. Gowri Ramnarayan, 'The endless road,' *Frontline*, 28 August 1992, 75.
17. Badal Sircar, *There's No End*, trans. K. Raha, *Enact*, Nov. 1971, 19.
18. Mohan Rakesh, *Perhaps*, trans. Bindu Batra, *Enact*, Aug.-Sept. 1973, 11.

Mental Deformity: Sircar's *Procession* and Tendulkar's *Encounter in Umbugland* and *Kanyadan*

> How colourful the processions are. Processions full of words and sounds. I'm lost in the colours of the banners carried in procession, the sounds of marching feet, I'm moving about lost, groping lost, I walk through roads and highways, the streams of humanity, through the bends, lost for ever. I've lost my way home. The way to my real home, my really real home.
>
> *Procession*

Human mind has also undergone division, differentiation and hierarchization since the dawn of civilization. The primal unity between rationality and intuition, the two faculties of mind, is lost. They are divided, differentiated and alienated. Hogie Wyckoff, a Transactional Analyst, observes that men are encouraged to develop their rationality and to suppress their intuition while women are encouraged to develop their intuition and to suppress their rationality.[1] This suits their roles imposed on them by sexist civilization as office work demands rationality while housework demands intuition. Similarly, intellectual professions demand rationality while manual jobs demand intuition so intellectuals possess overdeveloped rationality while workers possess overdeveloped intuition. This mental deformity not only thwarts awareness but also impairs the communication between men and women and between intellectuals and workers. And rationality is considered superior to intuition in our hierarchized society.

The function of rationality and intuition is severely maimed by lying, discounting the perception of reality, and drugs. Steiner exposes the invisible and widespread lying in his observation:

> Lying is the rule rather than exception in human affairs. We are all aware of the fact that we are being lied to by those who govern us, by the media as well as those who constantly attempt to convince us to spend our money on their products whether we need them or

> not. But we are less inclined to be aware of the fact that lying is more common than truth-telling in our everyday relationships.[2]

He then elaborates how we are trained to tell and accept lies by our parents, elders and teachers:

> So, as we grow into civilized adulthood we are fully prepared not only to be liars but to accept lies from others. It's a small wonder that people passively accept the lies of their elected officials, advertisers, and the media; their training to do so is relentless from early childhood on. . . . Lies in the schools are primarily by omission, though lies by commission also abound, especially when children are told outright lies about the functioning and administrative aspects of their school, their city, and their country. (158)

Evan D. Illich considers school worse than religion which Marx calls opiate. He discloses how school hampers our awareness instead of promoting it: "School seems eminently suited to be the World Church of our decaying culture. No institution could better veil from its participants the deep discrepancy between social principles and social reality in today's world."[3] Steiner uncovers the myth of 'truthfulness' taught to children at home and school: "'truthfulness,' as taught by grownups to children is simply a sophisticated way of lying as opposed to the crude, more simple way of lying which is punished." (159)

Parents, by example or injunction, unwittingly teach their children to get upset or confused and not to think when they face a problem. They often or always discount the rationality, the intuition and the feelings of their children, in addition to lying to them. Therefore, the children generally become mindless and even mad as they grow up. They also learn to discount and to accept discounting the truth. The process of making people mindless, in the family and the society, is successfully effected through religion, fine arts, mass media, education, unnatural ideals and drugs. This is succinctly elucidated in Badal Sircar's *Procession* and Vijay Tendulkar's *Encounter in Umbugland* and *Kanyadan*.

Sircar's *Procession* elucidates how mental deformity is effected and how it is perpetuated. The play has got neither a plot nor any characters in the conventional sense. Like *Stale News*, it is rather a collage of various episodes taken from the flux of human life. The underlying unity behind this heterogenous collection is the theme of 'being lost' in civilization. The characters are not types but representative and symbolic. They are Khoka, an Officer, and Old Man, a Master and a chorus of six people. Khoka and the Old Man form a group and the Officer and the Master, another. Khoka is killed and the Old Man is lost in the labyrinthine roads of the city.

> OLD MAN. Michhils, Michhils. I've lost my way. Through roads and roads I seek a road, through Michhils and Michhils I seek the road to my home.
>
> KHOKA. Everyday in the streets, in the streams of masses, I'm being pulverized under the stamping feet in processions, I'm dying, I'm being killed, Michhils.[4]

The city stands for civilization for which the Officer and the Master are custodians. The officer orders the people to start the procession (Michhil in Bengali) that represents various rituals of our civilization. He says: "Nobody's been killed. Nobody's lost. Everything's in order. Start it. Sta-a-art the procession." (17) People accept and obey masters. They believe that civilization does not exist without masters: "There will be wealth to ensure a good life for all men. But that will eliminate the Master, and all civilization will come to an end." (23) Conversely masters cannot exist without civilization and so they have to protect it for their own survival.

> THE MASTER. Who upholds, preserves and protects civilization?
>
> CHORUS. You, Master! (23)

In the play, Sircar aims at exposing the various devices of civilization in obscuring our awareness.

The play begins with an everyday happening of loadshedding in an Indian city. It is completely dark. A piercing death scream is heard. Some people light their matches and search for the victim. But they find none and one of them says: "They must've stabbed someone to death and whisked away the body." (5) There is a commotion and an Officer comes. He says: "Nobody was killed. Get back to your homes." (6) As he moves upto them threateningly, they sneak away. Then, Khoka comes and tries desperately to draw the attention of the Officer and the audience to himself. But the Officer does not notice him even when he comes right in front of him. Then Khoka says that he is killed everyday. Thus, the beginning of the play shows how the perception of the reality is completely discouraged with oppressive force.

Khoka screams again and falls down. The officer does not notice it and goes away. The Chorus comes singing a funeral song. Then, they carry the dead body of Khoka. Thus, the first procession in this play is a funeral. The Old Man comes and asks the people to join the procession. He, then, gives a list of various processions: "Michhils for food and clothes, Michhils for salvation, Michhils for the revolution, Michhils in military formation, Michhils of refugees, Michhils for flood relief, Michhils mourning, Michhils protesting, Michhils festive, Michhils with stars." (8)

As the play progresses, all these religious and revolutionary processions are acted. The inclusion of revolutionary processions in the list unfolds Sircar's own disillusionment with the existing Communist Parties and their movements. Gowri Ramnarayan also remarks: "The discovery that some respected leaders were liars and cheats who duped their followers led to disillusionment."[5] In the Introduction to *Three Plays*, Ella Dutta observes: "He does not wish to create new myths in place of the old. He prefers to raise the consciousness and create awareness of the issues." (viii) It is, thus, clear that Sircar does not intend to convey that the Communist Revolution is the real road to the real home.

The Old Man narrates how he, as a small boy, followed his father and how the criss-crossing roads were labyrinthine:

> I held on to my father's hands, as the road winded and meandered along and receded under my feet giving place to yet new roads. . . . All the roads vanished beyond the bend till a new road flashed at the bend till it vanished again at the next bend and a new one again and a bend and the vanishing road the new road the road the ro-o-o-o-ad. (8-9)

Then, all the people start searching for Khoka. They describe his features. In press and on radio and wireless, they announce that Khoka is lost. Khoka is coaxed to return and is offered various things such as bats, balls, biscuits, chocolates, books, college, pass, job, land, house, car, gold, happiness, peace and salvation. The Old Man, then, gives more information about him: "His parents named him Khoka. Thousands of parents with thousands of Khokas. Khoka means one who hasn't grown up yet. Khoka means Green, Raw, Immature." (10-11) The people call Khoka and request him to return home. The Old Man says that Khoka comes to the new home, the real home but not the old one. The words 'Khoka' and 'home' acquire a new meaning here. Khoka symbolizes a child who is not spoiled by civilization. He still possesses humanity. He is not dehumanized. He is an embodiment of humanity. The old home is the present society where humanity is constantly destroyed. The old home is not at all conducive to the survival of humanity. It is a dehumanizing environment where we vainly search for humanity. And the solution of one problem invariably leads to another problem and in seeking solutions, we encounter the same problem again in the present society. This is symbolically expressed by the Old Man as 'You go far and wide, you turn round and round, and come back to the same road.' (11) The new home is the future society where humanity is regained. It is free from dehumanizing civilization. Sircar portrays this real home in his play *Beyond the Land of Hattamala*.

One-day life of middle-class people in a city is then acted by the Chorus. People are on their way to work. They buy newspapers which are in the shape of fool's caps. This suggests the fooling of people by the press. Newspapers contain such news items as 'Conflict in the Middle East,' 'Train accident in Italy' and 'Examinations postponed again.' (12) They publish such statements of ministers and leaders as 'we should be prepared for more critical times' and 'Spiritualism alone can bring prosperity to the nation.' (12-13) Some people board trains and others take buses to go to work. Vendors sell various items and things on the train. For example, a salesboy sells pens. He advertises them in a fascinating manner:

> A Chinese pen of the same kind would have cost you eighteen rupees. But I offer you this pen for only one rupee. Only a rupee. If you buy three pens at a time you pay two rupees and fifty paise. . . . It's only on this train that you get a pen at this price. It's a very special publicity campaign by the company that brings you this pen for a rupee. (13)

Then in an overcrowded bus, people struggle to obtain 'a little space for a foot.' (14) They reach their workplace and become busy working. After work, they seek entertainment and relief by seeing a film or a match or playing a game. This shows how the people in cities are too busy with their routine life to use their mind properly and how passively their minds receive misleading news items, indoctrinating statements of popular leaders and false commercial advertisements. This is followed by the processions of various religions. Thus, the life of a man itself becomes a kind of procession, a ritual which is devoid of vitality or meaning.

Then, the Freedom Struggle is acted. The ambivalence of Indians to the British Government is shown:

> TWO. Remember, at the moment of your birth your life has been offered in sacrifice to the great mother.

THREE. Glory to the generous British government. (18)

After freedom, the communal riots take place. But freedom does not solve problems. The rich are prosperous and the poor are miserable. Middle-class people find life very hard as they have to buy rice, pulses, oil, sugar, kerosene, baby food and text books through black market. Potbellied profiteers dance and enjoy themselves. The poor and middle-class people are too intoxicated with their patriotism to protest against the exploitation. Most of them believe in what their leaders say eloquently. Master says:

> Remember our national heritage. Remember the numberless martyrs in our struggle for freedom. Remember the revolutionary heroes of our fiery days. Remember—India is the country of Manu, Parashar, Kalidas, Bhavabhuti, Sita, Savitri, Sri Chaitanya and Gandhiji. Remember the invincible strength of the principle of non-violence. Remember it's our responsibility to give spiritual leadership to the world. Remember the greatness of democracy in India. Remember the fundamental rights of the Constitution. Remember the Green Revolution, the Nationalization of Banks, Family Planning, the Dollar aid, the nuclear blast, arrests under Maintenance of Internal Security Act. (20-21)

Sircar exposes the myth of nationalism by juxtaposing it with the instances of exploitation and abject poverty.

Sircar does not blame any individual, any class or any government. He criticises the system. He incriminates civilization for all human misery. Civilization has caused all these deformities. The history of civilization is briefly stated by the Chorus:

ONE.	The Sun is a star in the Cosmos. The Earth is a planet of the Sun. Man is the greatest creature on Earth.
TWO.	All men were equal at the beginning of Creation. But they were uncivilized.
THREE.	Even with a whole hard day's work they didn't find food enough to fill their stomachs. So they were equal!
FOUR.	Then men learnt to use animals, they learnt agriculture. Then they had a surplus.
FIVE.	Surplus brought civilization. Man became civilized. Civilization civilized man, civilized society.

ONE.	Who would enjoy the surplus? Everyone? No. Only those who had quality, intelligence and force.
TWO.	The Master has quality, intelligence and force so the world has masters and slaves, will have masters and slaves. That's how the gods have laid it out . . . (22-23)

Inequality is an indispensable part of civilization and so egalitarianism destroys civilization. That is why the Master tells the people that Communism is the greatest enemy of civilization. Then he explains: "Rest assured, my children, I'll keep you civilized. Communism is the religion of the animals. Keep in mind that you are not animals, you are men." (23) Communism is attributed to animals as they are free from social deformity. Whatever may be the noble aims of religion, it is usually used to approve the oppressive and exploitative culture and to obscure awareness. That is why the Master advises the people to endure suffering to enter heaven after death when they complain about their miserable life: "There's heaven for you after you die, and heavenly happiness. Animals have no heaven. I bless you, you'd die as men, not animals." (24) This aptly illustrates the famous maxim of Marx that religion is an opiate.

After some time, the people again approach the Master as their suffering becomes too intense to be pacified by religious faith.

ONE.	Three years without a job, father's retired.
TWO.	It's the thirty-sixth day of the factory lockout. There's not a morsel at home.
THREE.	The untimely rain left all the rice rotting, our debts with the moneylender have risen to a mountain.
FOUR.	The whole family's laid up with food poisoning from adulterated cooking oil. I don't have the money to pay a doctor.
FIVE.	The police took my brother away, and beat him to death. (24)

They all say in Chorus: "O Master, we can't bear it any longer?" (24) Then, the Master gives them a bottle of liquor and advises them to drink it to forget their suffering. He says: "The elixir that will bring you oblivion." (25) They drink liquor and ironically say: "O Men! Let's be men." The Old Man also drinks and says: "Sura. Somarasa. Liquor. Daru. The best medicine. The way to lose oneself. Lose yourself, lose yourself, just get lost, stop searching." (25) Thus, people drink liquor and become mindless.

The Old Man's search for the real road to the real home symbolizes the search of mankind for the right way to regain their lost paradise, the primal bliss. So, the Old Man says: "I must've been walking for ages, and yet every time I get stuck here." (25) He gets lost and he tries various ways again and again. As he walks on in the drunken state, he meets Khoka who says that he is killed. Then, they both talk about themselves:

> KHOKA. I don't have a home. I had a home, now I don't have one. I'm killed.
>
> OLD MAN. You've just lost your way. Why do you have to be so round about? (28)

They, then, try to find out the way to their house. But they reach the same place where they have started. Meanwhile Khoka falls dead again. The Chorus takes his dead body in a funeral procession again.

The internalization of the values of deformed culture severely maims human mind. The internalized values form the *Master* in the mind of everybody. This internal *Master* is more harmful than the external *Master* as the former provides our deformed culture the resilience that it needs. That is why revolutions and reformist movements have failed to rectify the deformities of our culture and civilization. It is the internal *Master* in us that strongly objects to certain small positive changes in our society:

> ONE. This country needs military dictatorship. They should be all thrashed into order. (32)
>
> TWO. How could he marry that girl? A Brahman marrying a low caste? That's why they say: When it's love, one doesn't care whether it's this lowcaste or that!
>
> THREE. The lower classes are getting so impertinent. Even the rickshaw-wallahs put on airs. (32)
>
> ONE. Whips. They need whipping. Whips alone can straighten them.
>
> TWO. All the housewives are out on the streets, in jobs. What else do you need to bring morals to a finish?
>
> THREE. The servant demands higher wages. Ungrateful wretches! (33)

As long as this deformed thinking goes on, our mental deformity remains intact.

The Chorus starts singing a patriotic song:

> It's a fine world we live in, made of a jumble of spices.
> In the midst of it lies a land, the best most of all. . . .
> It's the best of all lands, the land of my birth. (33)

At once, Khoka runs in, followed by the Officer and says: "Stop it. stop fooling the people. It's not the truth. *(To the audience*) How can you tolerate it? Don't you see it's all lies? A fraud on you?" (33) The Officer shuts his mouth and carries him away. Then, the Master asks the officer to keep men happy and peaceful with fine arts:

> Keep men happy, in peace, and disciplined. Let people enjoy their lives. Give them art and culture. Art. Culture. Let people immerse themselves in a flow of aesthetic pleasure. When the dirty doubts surface, let the flow of pleasure wash over them. Keep in mind, men are not animals. Men alone can lose themselves in the flow of pleasure, sink into it. (34)

The Master, thus, uses various means of impairing human awareness such as nationalism, religion, liquor and finally fine arts. The people believe the Master and with reverence they carry him in a procession. They listen to his hypnotizing speech and the Officer also follows him slavishly.

The Old Man is disillusioned with processions and describes how he is fooled by various processions:

> How colourful the processions are. Processions full of words and sounds. I'm lost in the colours of the banners carried in procession, the sounds of marching feet, I'm moving about lost, groping lost. I walk through roads and highways, the streams of humanity, through the bends, lost for ever. I've lost my way home. The way to my real home, my really real home. (35)

Then, a revolutionary procession passes by and it is followed by some processions with meaningless slogans. Khoka is vexed and says: "Stop it, I don't believe in your processions. All processions have turned into processions of death, Death. Death alone." (37)

Then he illustrates his statements. There is a death from starvation in the world every six seconds. And millions of people are killed in wars all over the world every year. Khoka throws light on the collective responsibility of all the people in this ritual of killing one another: "You sit in peace watching murders, you are killed yourselves, you kill. Yes, you kill, you have killed. I'm killing, you are killing. We are all killers. We all kill, we all get killed. We kill by sitting quietly and doing nothing at ease, we get killed. Stop it. Stop it." (37) The Officer comes with five men, takes Khoka and kills him in various places in various ways.

The old man convinces Khoka that he is lost but not killed. He infuses hope in the young man. He asks him to lead him ahead. Finally, Khoka agrees to join the Old Man in his search for the real road to the real home. Then the old man hears a procession coming. He sees it approaching. He says, it is a real procession. He leads Khoka into the real procession where all the people hold one another's hands. Sircar does not describe the procession in detail. He says that it consists of men. Certainly, it does not represent any class or any party or any ideology. It is a human procession where all human beings, shedding the differences of caste, religion and nation, are united and where they collectively endeavour to solve all their problems. Veena Noble Dass remarks: "The spectators and actors intermingle and the entire space of the room becomes a swirling mass of humanity. It is one of those moments in the theatre when one becomes acutely aware of the possibilities of life and the essential brotherhood of man."[6]

Throughout the play, Khoka is killed and the Old Man is lost repeatedly. Khoka speaks the truth and symbolizes it. So, the killing of Khoka suggests the destruction of the truth. The Officer says that nobody is killed and disperses the people who witness the death of Khoka. This shows how the police force is used to prevent people from perceiving the truth. Similarly, nationalism, religion, liquor and entertainment are narcotically used by the Master to obfuscate the awareness of the people and to keep them mindless. The Old Man's inability to find the right road is due to his mindlessness caused by our cultural deformity.

Tendulkar's *Encounter in Umbugland* is equally concerned with mental deformity. India is traditionally called "Jambudwip" in Sanskrit and Tendulkar deliberately uses the word "Dambadwip." The rhyme in these two words intensifies the idea of hypocrisy. The English translation "Umbugland" which rhymes with "humbug" conveys the same idea effectively. The names of Vijaya, the Princess and Indira, the Prime Minister of India refer to one goddess, Lakshmi. The playwright draws parallels between the rule of Vijaya and that of Indira. In the Introduction to Tendulkar's *Five Plays*, Arundhati Banerjee rightly remarks: "It is not difficult to find reflections of the political situation in India of the late sixties and early seventies in the royalist regime of Dambadwip (Umbugland). . . . Despite the distancing achieved through the creation of a fictitious milieu, it is easy to identify the characters with political figures who held ministerial positions in those years."[7] The very life of politics is falsehood and hypocrisy and the political language becomes completely dishonest. As in India, in the play also, "Democracy has become a synonym for autocracy or dictatorship"[8] as observed by E. Renuka. Queen Vijaya introduces welfare schemes to strengthen her power. So there is more advertisement about the schemes than it is necessary. Prannarayan says to Vijaya: "They hear a lot of drumbeating about the Plan, but they don't get a sniff of their welfare in it."[9]

The play begins as Prannarayan invites the people to the sixtieth coronation anniversary of Vichitravirya, the king of Umbugland. He uses a beautiful euphemism to glorify the falsehood that they speak in their country. He talks about "three kinds of truth: conventional truth, diplomatic truth, and the real truth." (269) Then, two men enter, one from each wing, wielding huge pens like sceptres. They bang their pens on the ground three times, pronounce 'Victory' to the king and describe the ceremony of his sixtieth coronation anniversary. Each ritual is repeated sixty times. Prannarayan tells Vijaya, the Princess that "many have happily spent all their lives in this abode of luxury without bothering to think at all." (271) Vratyasom, being emotional, speaks the truth about politics while waiting for the king: "Let us not open our mouth too wide about the principles and honesty. To observe these two virtues in politics is as inappropriate and stupid as celibacy after marriage." (273)

As Vratyasom and other Ministers go on talking about politics, Vichitravirya, the King, arrives. He describes how eloquently he has spoken about various topics to the people who have listened to him with rapt attention. The Ministers hide their discontent and praise the king sycophantically:

PISHTAKESHI. His Majesty is the sole artist of the island's destiny.

VRATYASOM. His majesty is Umbugland and Umbugland is His Majesty. (277)

Vichitravirya believes this and affirms it: "We have become so much one with Umbugland in these past sixty years, and our people of Umbugland have so identified themselves with us, that the thought of one without the other is impossible." (277) He is confident that he will live another hundred years and thinks that the island badly needs his leadership for at least another fifty years. The Ministers go on increasing the period of his rule from fifty years to five hundred years.

Vichitravirya intuitively knows the ambition of his ministers to capture power after him. He says to them:

> There is not in any of you in the slightest measure the capacity to hold the reins of government in this island after us. Even though the responsibilities of government have been divided amongst you, it is still we who take all the decisions. Besides, there is no unity amongst you. . . . Power seems more important to you than duty! Selfish designs have replaced service! . . . We have not cherished a lust for power even for one second. . . . If that is your only desire, take it, with pleasure . . . take it this minute! We will abdicate, and become a hermit. . . . But our people will not release us. It is according to their wish, their pleasure, according to what their wish and will shall be that we shall stay in power. With this aim, we have planned to undergo an experiment in rejuvenation. Only today we have received medical advice as a result of which we shall be able to rule for at least a hundred years. (278-79)

He advises his Ministers to serve the people selflessly and to let him rule the country. As he speaks, he poses for the painter to paint his picture. Vijaya, his daughter, urged by Prannarayan, comes and congratulates him. She says that her father looks decrepit and old when he asks Aranyaketu how he looks in his royal costumes. He lies dead in the pose that he is as the painter finishes his painting. All are shocked by the sudden death of the king. The two pen-bearers, clothed in black, sing a funeral song mournfully:

> Darkness at the height of day.
> Umbugland in deep dismay.
> Sun sinks in gloom.
> Umbugland becomes a tomb. (282)

A great question is asked everywhere, 'After Vichitravirya, Who?' It reminds us of the question of late sixties in India, 'After Nehru, Who?'

There are five Ministers in the Cabinet: Pishtakeshi from the West, Karkashirsha from the North, Aranyaketu from the North-East, Vratyasom from the East and Bhagadanta. Each Minister wants to occupy the throne and brings some people to support him. The two pen-bearers describe the strengths and weaknesses of each minister. All the

Ministers meet and discuss but fail to come to a conclusion unanimously. The political crisis feeds the press with sensational news. Finally the crisis is resolved when all the Ministers choose Vijaya to be the Queen, the heiress of Vichitravirya. They all plan to rule the country in her name.

Prannarayan takes pains to train Vijaya in ruling the country. He teaches her political diplomacy. He says to her: "One should take stock of the situation—give some advantages, and get some. Politics means sweetly-smiling enmity and the experience of sacrifice. A show of sacrifice is always profitable in politics." (306) He instructs her how to be diplomatic in her relations with others. He enlightens her on the psychology of the people: "Each of them is more important than the next. One must insult them so lightly that their self-importance won't suffer." (299) Vijaya at first does not like the responsibility and wants to enjoy life spontaneously: "I don't think I can manage. I feel like dancing, laughing and singing. I feel like playing and running about! Sometimes, Prannarayan, I even feel like shouting loudly without any reason." (298) Prannarayan then says: "With all due respect to piety and health, this is just human nature! But it doesn't do for a ruler to be human. He has to be superhuman, or even divine." (298) Thus, it is clear that one should not be true to oneself in politics. One has to become dehumanized and mentally deformed. During the first Cabinet meeting, the Child in Vijaya cries for freedom. She questions: "What crime did I commit, that I've been imprisoned in the palace since childhood?" Gradually, she learns enjoying power and succeeds in suppressing the humanity in her.

Vijaya agrees to the three proposals of the Ministers. Later, she meets various people and gives a suitable message to each. The two pen-bearers report her activities and adore her. She mingles with tribal people and launches a plan to uplift them. She outwits her Ministers in diplomacy and becomes more popular than they. They feel, "the pranks Vijaya has been up to recently are a challenge to the authority of the Cabinet." (311) They wanted to enjoy power by making a pawn of Vijaya but she started making pawns of them. Now they realise: "We placed her on the throne, and now she wants to plant one foot firmly on it and the other on us!" (312) They unanimously resent Vijaya's independent functioning without consulting the Cabinet. They decide to give the Queen a strong reminder of their existence.

The two pen-bearers report the successful completion of the first year of Vijaya's rule. Vijaya romantically explains to Prannarayan about her plans to uplift the people of Kadamba tribe: "This plan will raise my stature on the island. I will get the credit for achieving what has never been achieved before. This plan will make everyone understand that I am not just my father's daughter, nor a puppet ruler. From now on I plan to rule in earnest." (317) Meanwhile the Ministers arrive and she welcomes them cordially. She takes the trouble of explaining to them her plan of uplifting the people of Kadamba tribe. But they ridicule her plans in every possible way. Yet, she does not lose her patience. She requests them to sign their names on the plan so that she may start implementing it at once. Nobody likes her plan and everybody walks out. She expresses her resentment to Prannarayan who exposes her hidden motive.

VIJAYA.	(*angrily*) My motives are pure! I want to givc status to the poor people of this island.
PRANNARAYAN.	Perhaps thereby your Highness wishes to increase your own! The motive of improving your own position on this Island may also be hidden behind this pure motive. (325)

She declares emergency and implements her plans to uplift the poor because the Ministers have not approved of them. The two pen-bcarers report the incidcnts and discuss the future encounter between the Queen and the Cabinet in Umbugland.

Vijaya conveys through Prannarayan to the Ministers that she is going to put the plan into operation on her own authority. The Ministers feel that this royal decree is tantamount to proclaiming that they are a puppet Cabinet. They arc cnraged and discuss how they can teach her a lesson. Vratyasom takes active role in the discussion. He says:

> Wc must incite the people! We must loose upon her the tidal wave of an infuriated mob. That's what'll rock her! She's still raw, she's an inexperienced child. She's calling like a jackal; she hasn't as yet seen the angry roaring tiger of the mob. Brave men tremble when they see this fourteenth wonder of the world rushing towards them, shouting till throats are hoarse, attacking with stones. What's a raw girl going to do? (334)

When Karkashirsha says that he does not know any people, Vratyasom tells him how they can buy people through agents for a rebellion. Aranyaketu asks whether this will lead to bloodshed and destruction. Vratyasom replies that it is inevitable to effect a change. Bhagadanta does not agree to the encounter that kills people. When he is gone, Pishtakeshi says that a battle with the Queen is inevitable. The Vratyasom explains his plan of action: "At least fifty martyrs must sacrifice their lives. Property worth at least five or seven hundred thousand must be wrecked." (337) Even in their plan, they are not united. The two pen-bearers describe the encounter between the Queen and the Ministers.

Bhagadanta is a Kadamba and does not support other Ministers who are against the Queen's plan to uplift the Kadamba people. He secretly conveys to the Queen the plans of the Ministers to incite the people against her. Vijaya successfully plans her counter-attack. Pran-narayan describes the arrangements:

> All the arrangements have been completed according to your Majesty's command. Armed guards are already hidden in every window of the palace. More guards are concealed in convenient houses near the palace square. Famished criminals in Kadamba costume have been stuffing their bellies with food behind the palace for the past two days. And a host of burglars, thieves and pick-pockets, disguised as the common people, have been let loose in the palace precincts on daily wages. Their misconduct has sorely harassed the genuine populace. Of course, our spies, disguised as servants, have penetrated the households of each of the Ministers. (342-43)

The two pen-bearers describe the demands of the Ministers and the details of their attack.

Vratyasom and other Ministers wait for the Queen in the palace. They are happy about their arrangements. A fierce fight goes on between the people and the soldiers. Vijaya comes and asks the Ministers to go to the people and know their demands. They say that they know the demands.

> VRATYASOM. 'Stop the Kadamba Plan!'
> PISHTAKESHI. 'Give the Ministers back their power!'
> KARKASHIRSHA. And 'Abdicate!'

Vijaya does not believe them and sends Bhagadanta to the people who kill him. Thus, she shows that angry people always lose discrimination. The Ministers feel frightened. The uncontrollable mob is ready to burn down the palace. Then, Vijaya herself goes out to face the people. The Ministers think that she will be killed by the furious crowd. The people throw stones and a few soldiers are injured lethally. Queen Vijaya addresses them boldly and orders them to be quiet. She says whatever comes to her mind and they express their applause. Having gained confidence, she announces that she will abolish taxation. Yet, they are silent. Then, she goes on talking about her future activities: "We shall institute a public enquiry into the private property of our Ministers, who have today gone against the interests of the people. . . . Those Ministers who are found guilty will be severely punished." (353) This cheers the people. She shouts, 'Down with the Cabinet.' And they shout it back louder than she. When a few people demand her to scrap the Kadamba Plan, she shouts, "Down with the Plan—*and the Ministers who made it!*" (354) Then, they shout, "Death to each Minister." The Ministers understand the gravity of the situation and surrender to Queen Vijaya who saves them tactically.

All the people in the play tell lies to one another. And the falsehood is translated into their behaviour, resulting in hypocrisy. They allow themselves to be dehumanized in order to enjoy power. In their scramble for power, they lose peace and happiness. Not only the rulers but also the ruled are mentally deformed. They blindly believe their leaders. Prannarayan, a eunuch, is the only person who perceives the reality as rightly pointed out by Veena Noble Dass. (127) Towards the end of the play, he criticises the credulous people:

> I see you upside down, a formless, characterless, lifeless, existenceless gathering. The blind, deaf and dumb spectators of the whole encounter—who allow men to become politicians, politicians to become statesmen, statesmen to become cunning, and cunning men to become robots, mechanical men. You are a force that claps its hands, makes strange noises with its mouth, an amazing untiring force— (356)

The play thus shows how leaders make people mindless and how mindless people allow their leaders to be hypocritical. It discloses how a great damage can be caused by mental deformity.

Tendulkar's play, *Kanyadan*, recently published in English, illustrates the mental deformity of an Indian woman caused by her own father. In pursuing the ideal of her father, the protagonist discounts the hard reality and risks her marital life. Finally, she realizes the truth and tells her father in his face how he crippled her mind by setting unrealistic ideals.

Nath Devalikar and Seva are the parents of Jyoti and Jayaprakash. They are socialists and have worked hard for dalits for a long time. Jyoti inherits her father's idealism and loves Arun Athavali, a dalit poet, whom she meets at the Socialist study group. She puts forward her decision to marry Arun before her parents and brother. Nath feels very happy and says: "But if my daughter had decided to marry into high caste, it wouldn't have pleased me much."[10] But Seva intuitively apprehends the misery that may follow this marriage and forewarns Jyoti about it. When her intention is misunderstood, she clarifies herself to Jyoti: "My anxiety is not over his being a dalit. You know very well that Nath and I have been fighting untouchability tooth and nail, God knows since when. So that's not the issue. But your life has been patterned in a certain manner. You have been brought up in a specific culture. To erase or to change all this overnight is not just possible. He is different in every way. You may not be able to handle it." (13) But Jyoti fails to see sense in Seva's forewarning and firmly syas: "I will manage, mother!" (13) The final decision is postponed till they see Arun.

When Arun comes to Jyoti's house, she is alone. The feelings of inferiority, that he has acquired in the dalit environment imposed by our hierarchized society, surface in his mind and make him uncomfortable in this big Brahmin house. So he requests Jyoti to be with him when she is about to go into the kitchen to make some tea for him. As she requests him to accompany her to the kitchen, the male chauvinist in him comes out and says: "men who sit and chat in the kitchen are pansies!" (17) Jyoti feels shocked yet she ignores it. Arun feels challenged when she discounts his statement that he will beat his wife. So he twists her arm and she feels more shocked than hurt. Yet she ignores it.

Jyoti introduces Arun to her brother and later her mother. She goes into the kitchen to make some tea when Seva talks to Arun. He feels nervous and bored. So, he makes her restless by being discourteous. He tells her that he can earn good money by brewing illicit liquor. When Jayaprakash comes, he repeats this to make him feel awkward: "I was telling her about this matter of brewing illicit liquor. [*with determined obstinacy.*] So I was saying that this business is highly profitable. Secondly, it is fun for the man and wife. Can take it easy. If there are children, there's work for them also, to wash glasses and plates, to fetch *paan* and cigarettes." (21) Jyoti vainly tries to alleviate the situation by saying that Arun is joking. She adds that she knows everything about him. But he says to her, in the presence of her mother: "You don't know a shit. Shut up." (21) The tension reaches its climax when Nath arrives.

Nath behaves very courteously with Arun who does not reciprocate his warm feelings. Yet, he praises Arun and expresses his great joy over realizing his ideal of breaking the caste barriers through the marriage of Jyoti to Arun. When Arun leaves, Seva and Jayaprakash complain about Arun's rude behaviour. But Nath ignores their accusation and justifies Jyoti's decision to marry Arun. He says:

> He may not be a gentleman, but neither is he a scoundrel. As a human being he has potential. He has intelligence, drive and creativity. He has come so far despite his circumstances. This is not an easy matter. It is the result of his effort and dedication. You cannot imagine at what cost these people have made little progress that they have. He is unrefined gold, he needs to be melted and moulded. This is the need of the hour. Who can perform this task if not girls like Jyoti? (13)

Thus Jyoti gets Nath's moral support and marries Arun.

Jyoti works and earns while Arun spends it. He often gets drunk and beats her mercilessly. When she cannot bear it any longer, she comes to her parents's house. Nath attributes Arun's cruelty to his despair due to their lack of residence. So, he offers a room in his house for Jyoti and Arun. But Jyoti says that she has left him as she was fed up with him. She sobs uncontrollably. Seva and Jayaprakash support Jyoti. But Nath does not give up his ideal: "(*with passion.*) Seva, let not this wonderful experiment fail! This dream which is struggling to turn real, let it not crumble into dust beforc our eyes! We have to do something. We must save this marriage." (41) Then, Arun himself comes and apologizes for his cruel behaviour. But Seva is not convinced of his apology and questions him why he has beaten Jyoti. This leads to an argumcnt between them:

> ARUN: What am I but the son of scavengers. We don't know the non-violent ways of brahmins like you. We drink and beat our wives . . . we make love to them . . . but the beating is what gets publicized . . .
>
> SEVA: Jyoti is not used to this kind of barbarism.
>
> ARUN: I am what I am . . . and shall remain exactly that. And your Jyoti knew what I was even before she married me. In spite of that she married me, she did it out of her own free will.
>
> SEVA: She thought you would improve after marriage.
>
> ARUN: If she thought so your Jyoti is a stupid fool. (44)

Nath intervenes and breaks up the argument. Jyoti goes with Arun. Seva breaks down while Nath feels proud of his daughter and says: "The training I gave you has not been in vain." (45)

Arun publishes his autobiography which receives a good acclamation. Nath praises it. "Such a powerful autobiography. Hats off to Arun Rao!" (46) He learns from Seva how cruelly Arun beats and kicks Jyoti in spite of her being pregnant. He cannot comprehend his split personality: "Such behaviour towards a pregnant wife! What happens if she dies? Such heinous behaviour by someone who wrote this beautiful autobiography." (47) Seva cannot control herself any longer and bursts before Nath: "The truth is that your dalit son-in-law, who can write such a wonderful autobiography, and many lovely poems, wants to remain an idler. He wants his wife to work. And with her money he wants to drown himself in drink, and have a hell of time with his friends. On top of that, for entertainment, he wants to kick his wife in the belly." (47-48) Nath also gets upset and enraged and says: "in this excellent book, whatever the author has said about injustice and exploitation is hypocrisy of the first order." (49) Later Jayaprakash joins the discussion. By quoting the news item that the Jews who were once persecuted have now become the merciless murderers of Palestinians, he infers that "yesterday's Victim is today's Victimizer," (51) only to hint at the persecution of Jyoti, a Brahmin lady, by Arun, a dalit youth. Meanwhile Arun himself comes along with his two friends. He requests Nath to talk about his book in the meeting. When Nath politely refuses, he blackmails him by saying that as his name is included in the list of speakers, the people will say: "the rise of the dalit son-in-law to the literary heights caused heartburn in the upper caste, socialist father-in-law," (55) if he does not speak. Arun and his friends leave as Nath does not yield to this. But Seva advises him to concede to Arun's request because she fears, "If we go against his wishes, it will mean more suffering for Jyoti." (57-58)

Nath praises Arun's book. Yielding to his blackmailing though he detests his hypocrisy. As he comes home, he is tormented by his conscience. Jayaprakash and Seva vainly try to pacify him. In utter despair, he blames himself for the misery of his daughter: "If she has committed any crime it is this: she took her father's words for gospel truth. She adopted her father's values." (62) Then, Seva forces him to go in and have rest. Later, Jyoti comes and expresses her desire to speak to Nath. Her formal behaviour astonishes Jayaprakash and Seva. When Nath comes, she takes him to task for his dishonest speech and does not accept his justification. Finally, she accuses him of making her mentally crippled: "Someone said these people kidnap little children, break their limbs and make them cripples. Bhai, forgive me for my words, but you have made us. (*She cannot go on.*)" (69-70) She orders everybody not to visit her house.

Jyoti thus becomes mindless and surrenders to the situation. She, like her father, plays the Rescuer while Arun plays the Victim. Her role prevents her from perceiving the reality. Her rescuing, at first, makes him behave more helplessly and then triggers his feelings of inferiority.

Consequently, he shifts to the role of Persecutor in order to feel powerful and beats Jyoti mercilessly. Jyoti goes down to the role of Victim. Thus, the Rescuer-Victim transaction ends up as the Persecutor-Victim transaction. This Drama Triangle makes not only Jyoti but also Arun mindless. Arun is very cruel because he becomes heartless as well as mindless to feel powerful. The unreal idealism of Nath and Jyoti reflects their favourite role of rescuing which impairs their perception of the reality. The play was branded anti-dalit by such critics as Vijay Tapas.[11]

Sircar's *Scandal in Fairyland* elucidates the crucial role of the press in moulding the public opinion though it is a funny tale for children. Midas Speculatorotti runs Daily Fairy Green, the largest circulated daily in Fairyland. As his name suggests, whatever business he does turns out to be very successful (gold). He contrives a new plan to earn gold and wealth in plenty very easily. A prince and an ogre become pawns in his commercial game. The Ogre is old and weak yet he frightens people in a kingdom. The king announces that he will give half his kingdom and his daughter to the hero who slays the ogre. Prince Thunderbolt goes to the ogre and pretends to kill him who actually disappears from the kingdom. The Princess accepts half the kingdom and takes gold instead of the princess. Midas takes thirty percent of the reward. This is repeated in another kingdom. Thus, this has happened in six kingdoms: Goldlandis, Silver State, Pearl Kingdom, Diamond Isle, Emeraldia and Land of Gems.

The people read Daily Fairy Green and believe the stories published in it. Now they learn about the seventh adventure of Prince Thunderbolt in Copperland:

> FOUR. The voice of the people of Fairyland, the daily Fairy Green—
> ONE. congratulates Prince Thunderbolt on his decision,
> TWO. worthy of a brave and true knight.
> THREE. It is our hope that Prince Thunderbolt will for ever remain loyal to his mission,
> FOUR. and save more such kingdoms from the onslaughts of ogres.[12]

They do not realize why Daily Fairy Green highlights Prince Thunderbolt's adventures. They feel thrilled to read about the nobility of the Prince. Midas through his daily develops such a kind of reputation around the Prince as entraps him. For example, the Paperboy says, "Sacred vow to save Fairyland—the bachelor prince's noble ideals—

sacrifices connubial bliss for love of Fairyland." (38) Prince Thunderbolt receives a call from Ironia. The paperboy announces while selling Daily Fairy Green:

> Daily Fairy Green! Daily Fairy Green! Ogre threatens Ironia—Demands one human a day—King proclaims half the kingdom and hand of Princess Rose—Beautiful, educated, honey-voiced, well versed in royal duties—you'll get her picture in this Daily Fairy Green! Extra . . . (38)

King Ironheart feels happy that Prince Thunderbolt has killed the eighth ogre. The Prince loves Princess Rose and agrees to marry her. Midas does not like this as it will end his business of earning gold easily. So, his daily criticises the Prince and then exposes the fraud:

> If a prince and a hero of the distinction of Prince Thunderbolt stoops to place his personal comfort and happiness over considerations of nation and state, like just any Tom, Dick or Harry, can the nation expect anything more from him? (42)
>
> ONE. (*reading*) One hears that Prince Thunderbolt has killed many an ogre in different countries in Fairyland.
>
> TWO. (*reading*) But has anyone ever seen a single one of these dead ogres? (43)

Consequently, the people demand a proof from the Prince. On the advice of Thunderbolt, the King arranges a trial. The ogre confesses the truth and Midas is forced to admit his guilt. The Minister sentences Midas to exile. Thunderbolt marries Rose and the tale ends happily. The play shows how the press is used to influence the minds of the masses for the growth of business. Sircar's *Stale News* also exemplifies how people are made confused and mindless by education, press and mass media as already discussed in the third chapter.

Mad Delight[13] by Mohan Rakesh portrays the landscape of the mind of the modern man. The play resembles Beckett's *Waiting for Godot*. It shows the activities of a man with a multicoloured mushroom. The sound and the light play a major role in the play and they almost become the very characters of the play. The sound of a stengun is heard whenever the man touches the mushroom. The sound, the change of lights and the actions of the man indicate the changing relationship between the mushroom and the man as rightly observed by Veena Noble Dass. (40) The play demonstrates how our mind becomes fragmented as we try to adapt ourselves to the varied complex surroundings. Rakesh explains his idea of 'today's mood of life' to Maharishi:

> Today's reality is something that is becoming increasingly complex. Something is constantly happening to us and in our desperate effort to strike an equilibrium with the surroundings. We are making constant adjustments. Everyone of us is living a life in fragments. During the course of one single day one is forced to play ten different parts and sometimes more than one version of each part. What remains constant is one's sense of being; the idea of a crisis. It is this that I call today's mood of life. And it is in this sense that one feels fragmented.[14]

Thus, life has become a drama as men act the roles which are alien to their real nature and which are imposed on them by sociocultural environment. The isolation of the identity of the sound from that of the visual, in the play, reflects the schizophrenic state of the present day human mind.

Parents, elders, teachers, leaders, religious preachers and business people go on telling lies by omission and commission and discounting the rationality and intuition of their children, students and people. This cultural programming in mindlessness begins at birth and continues throughout life. The mindlessness of people sustains other cultural deformities. In Sircar's *Procession* and *Stale News*, people are made mindless through nationalism, religion, liquor, press, mass media, education and entertainment to sustain the exploitative and oppressive culture. The Queen in Tendulkar's *Encounter in Umbugland* and Midas in Sircar's *Scandal in Fairyland* make use of press to sustain her rule and his business respectively. In Tendulkar's *Kanyadan*, Nath and Jyoti become mindless in playing the Rescuer whereas Arun becomes a mindless persecutor in order to overcome his inner feelings of inferiority. Mohan Rakesh's *Mad Delight* depicts the morbid mind of the modern man.

NOTES

1. Hogie Wyckoff, "Sex Role Scripting in Men and Women," *Scripts People Live*, Claude M. Steiner (New York: Bantam, 1980) 196-209.
2. Steiner, *Scripts People Live*, 155.
3. *Deschooling Society* (Harmondsworth: Penguin, 1973) 48.

4. Badal Sircar, *Procession,* trans. Samik Bandyopadhyay, *Three Plays* (Calcutta: Seagull, 1985) 16.
5. Gowri Ramnarayan, "The endless road of Badal Sircar's 'free theatre,' *Frontline*, 28 August 1992, 75.
6. *Modern Indian Drama in English Translation* (New Delhi: n.p, 1988) 72.
7. (Bombay: Oxford UP, 1992) x.
8. "All About Umbugland: A Study of Vijay Tendulkar's Plays," Diss. Kakatiya U, 1984, 147.
9. Vijay Tendulkar, *Encounter in Umbugland*, trans. Priya Adarkar, *Five Plays* (Bombay: Oxford UP, 1992) 344.
10. Vijay Tendulkar, *Kanyadan* (Delhi: Oxford UP, 1996) 8.
11. Vijay Tapas, "Tendulkar: The Number Two Anti-Dalit," *Adhikar Raksha* (Bulletin of the Committee for Protection of Democratic Rights, Bombay) VI: 1 and 2, Jan.-June 1983.
12. Badal Sircar, *Beyond the Land of Hattamala* and *Scandal in Fairyland*, trans. Suchanda Sarkar (Calcutta: Seagull, 1992) 37.
13. Mohan Rakesh, *Mad Delight*, *Enact,* No. 66. June 1970.
14. Mohan Maharishi, "Changing Role of Words in Theatre: Mohan Rakesh," *Sangeet Natak*, No. 22, Oct.-Dec. 1971, 26.

Spiritual Deformity: Rakesh's *The Great Swans of the Waves*, Sircar's *Bhoma* and Tendulkar's *The Vultures*

There's the taste of Bhoma's blood on the tongue. We drink Bhoma's blood, and laugh and play. There's blood dripping down the sides of our mouths, dripping, dripping, the poisonous plants are growing, growing. My blood, man's blood, becomes cold, c-o-l-d, c-o-l-d. . .

Bhoma

Girish Karnad, talking about angst in his writing, remarks: "I think anxiety has become part of existence today, triggered partly by the endemic violence. In India, the more we claim we are a spiritual people, the more violent we seem to get."[1] Usually, violence is attributed to animal impulses. But animals are not so violent and so destructive as human beings. Erich Fromm, having studied human destructiveness, argues:

> The study of animals shows that mammals and especially primates—although possessing a good deal of defensive aggression, are not killers and torturers. Paleontology, anthropology, and history offer ample evidence against the instinctivistic thesis: (1) human groups differ so fundamentally in the respective degree of destructiveness that the facts could hardly be explained by the assumption that destructiveness and cruelty are innate; (2) various degrees of destructiveness can be correlated to other physical factors and to differences in respective social strutures, and the degree of destructiveness increases with increased development of civilization, rather than the opposite.[2]

In course of civilization, human soul also undergoes division, differentiation and polarization and the polarized fragments of human soul become alienated and antagonistic. This leads to spiritual deformity which manifests itself in human violence and destructiveness.

'Soul' is an abstract word and it has several meanings. Here the word is used to mean the innermost core of human mind. For Freud, it is the Id which consists of life and death impulses, symbolized by Eros and Thanatos. Indian equivalent gods are Madana (love) and Rudra (death). The Hindu myth of Madana[3] symbolically reveals the inner conflict of human soul. Once Rudra renounces all worldly pleasures and begins performing rigorous penance. Other gods seek the help of Madana to instigate love in Rudra whose son alone can slay Tarakasura, a demon, who is tormenting them. Madana concedes to their request and stimulates love in Rudra. Being disturbed, Rudra is enraged and burns Madana by opening his third eye. Later, realizing the truth, he grants the wish of Rati, Madana's wife and revives Madana without any body.

Norman O. Brown makes an elaborate study of this aspect in *Life against Death.*[4] He recognises three phases of human history in this regard. In the first phase, life and death impulses were in the undifferentiated primal unity. Then, human beings enjoyed life happily and peacefully. In course of civilization, life and death impulses have been divided, differentiated and polarized. They have therefore become alienated and antagonistic. All human history is only the manifestation of their conflict. In this conflict, they repress each other and impose restriction on each other. Consequently, human beings can neither enjoy life completely nor renounce it fully. So, they have become mentally ill. This is the second phase. When they realize the real cause of their misery, they strive for reunification. In this phase, life and death impulses become undifferentiated and get reunified in final unity. Talking about love and renunciation of life, Rajneesh points out: "Both these ways have failed. The East has failed because it tried meditation without love. The West has failed because it tried love without meditation. My whole effort is to give you a synthesis, the whole—which means meditation plus love."[5]

Claude M. Steiner looks at this issue from another angle, the angle of Transactional Analysis. All human beings need love and recognition for their survival. Originally, they are capable of loving and being loved spontaneously. But this capability has been progressively impaired in course of civilization and lovelessness has been oppressively used to make people conform to exploitative culture. Steiner, therefore, observes: "The end result is that the capacity to love is taken away from people and then directed against them by using it as a reinforcer to bring about desired behaviour."[6] He argues that an artificial scarcity for love is created and that a rationed supply of love is supplied to love-starved people in order to control them in a desired manner. People are enjoined not to love others, not to ask for love, not to accept love from others and not to love themselves. Moreover, free exchange of love is prevented by heterosexual and homosexual taboos. People who love one another unconditionally cannot exploit and oppress one another. All these elements of spiritual deformity are found in Mohan Rakesh's *The Great Swans of the Waves*, Badal Sircar's *Bhoma* and Vijay Tendulkar's *The Vultures*

The Great Swans of the Waves begins with an epigraph quoted from Ashvaghosha's *Saundarananda* from which Rakesh borrows his theme. The epigraph epitomizes the theme of the play:

> Not the Buddha's austere path
> nor his wife's love attracts
> one uncertain his way
> like the great swans of the waves.[7]

The title of the play borrowed from the poem is suggestive. In *Saundarananda*, Nand overcomes his fascination for Sundari, his beautiful wife and seeks salvation in Buddhism. But Rakesh makes the character of Nand represent the modern man who like the great swans on the waves wavers between the two options: love and renunciation.

As the curtain raises, we see people busy with preparations for the Feast of God of Love (Madana) and hear the chant of Buddhist monks:

> Dhammam sharanam gachchami.
> Sangham sharanam gachchami.
> Buddham sharanam gachchami. (1)

Thus, the aura of the theme is set at the beginning itself. And this is intensified with the introduction of two polarized characters: Shwetang and Shyamang. Shwetang is gay and agile as his name suggests (Shwetang—white body); Shyamang is gloomy and meditative as his name suggests (Shyamang—black body). Shwetang is busy looking after the preparations while Shyamang being obsessed with thinking cannot do a thing and talks to himself. "Leave the leaves to Shyamang . . . what if Shyamang can't separate the leaves? Won't the love feast go on as planned? . . . Shwetang says don't think. But is thinking or not thinking a matter of will and pleasure?" (2) Then, Alka's dream and Sundari's desire reflect the same dichotomy. Alka sees a dry lake, a leafless tree and the leaden sky in her morning dream whereas Sundari is looking forward to a great love feast. Sundari tells Alka that if Lady Yashodhara could have bound Prince Siddhartha, he would not have become a saint. But she does not foreknow that her charming beauty fails to prevent

Nanda from being influenced by Buddha.

Sundari understands the mental state of Shyamang and asks him to leave his work to somebody and go. He goes to the lake and watches the shadows of the swans on the lake. He throws several stones at them and the swans feel frightened. They cry out loudly and fly away. Their cry disturbs Sundari who sentences Shyamang to solitary confinement in a dungeon for hurting the innocent birds. Then she learns that Alka loves him and wonders how he is loved by Alka. Meanwhile, Nand comes and takes two gulps of wine. He tells Sundari that he is tired because he has chased a deer. He describes how the deer has died:

> Not just escaped. It's not so much physical weariness as mental. The fact that the deer was not wounded by my arrow did not hurt my mind so much as seeing him, when I was returning tired and dispirited, lying dead a little distance down the road. (4)

The incident shows the state of Nand's mind. Nand informs Sundari that all the guests may not turn up as they are visiting Yashodhara who is going to become a nun. But Sundari is still hopeful of receiving a few guests. Meanwhile, she orders Shwetang to release Shyamang and to look after him well as she has promised Alka. She realizes that nobody is coming to the feast when Maitreya informs her about other guests. She feels greatly frustrated and dejected. Yet, she says: "I'm the cause of my own disturbance. I don't give anyone else the right to be the cause of my disturbance." (6) The Buddhist influence is so powerful that everything goes against Sundari's feast of love. People are fascinated more by Yashodhara's renunciation than by the love-feast of Sundari. The First Act foreshadows the future events.

Sundari falls asleep on the swing chair. Nand is worried about her great disappointment and so cannot sleep. Shyamang babbles in a state of delirium. Nand asks Alka to take care of him. He then thinks of Sundari's great frustration and talks about her changing feelings: "How cold and hard and bright you were when you were in a temper! And how tender, helpless and innocent in sleep! How like that deer which I left fallen in the forest yesterday! So long as it was daring us to run after it, it, too, was bright and fleeting." (7)

Sundari is as spontaneous as the deer in her feelings. So, she is able to sleep in spite of her disappointment. Nand is too obsessed with feelings to sleep. Sundari feels sorry for Shyamang and allows Alka to look after him. She asks Nand to help her toilette. She is annoyed by his obsession with the deer and orders him to hold the mirror for her as a punishment. She goes about her toilette as he holds the mirror. A little later, a Chorus chants the Buddhist prayer. Being disturbed by it, Nand drops the mirror without knowing it. Sundari is shocked and hurt. He requests her to forgive him. She asks him whether he is disturbed by the chant of the mendicants, one of whom may be Yashodhara. But he denies it. He is again disturbed by the sounds of a wind and some birds. Then Sundari explains the difference between them.

SUNDARI. You're being oversensitive.
NAND. *(comes down)* You don't find anything extraordinary in it?
SUNDARI. I don't look for extraordinary meanings in ordinary things. (10)

Then Alka comes and says that Shyamang is in a coma. She informs that Buddha and other mendicants came for alms to Nand's house. Nand feels guilty for not responding to their call for alms. He requests her to permit him to visit Buddha and promises her that he will return soon. She asks him to put a mark of planet on her forehead. When he puts it, she says that she will do the rest of her toilette after he returns. She adds that she will not let him sleep as a punishment if he fails to return soon. Her toilette remains incomplete.

The Second Act symbolically shows how love is frustrated at every stage in life. Rakesh himself talks about Shyamang: "Shyamang is a symbolic character. In a way he is a graphic description of the overactive mind that Nand has. His madness is really the mental imbalance created by too much thinking."[8] N.C. Jain, discussing the theme of the play, points out: "The first Act centres around Sundari in which Nand is merely her charmed and admiring husband. In the second Act, the focus shifts to his inner conflict, though its outline is still very dim."[9] It is interesting to note that Nand loses his balance of mind whereas Sundari remains relatively calm and peaceful in spite of her being frustrated again.

Sundari is worried about missing swans. She wonders how the swans have left the sanctuary. She tells Alka why she has allowed Nand to visit Buddha: "When I sent him away, it was with a certain trust. I could have stopped him if I wanted. But I didn't stop him, because it would have been weak of me to do so. And now I'm happy to think that, whatever weakness there was, it was none of mine." (11) She wonders why Nand has not returned yet. But she does not want to send anybody for him. It is already very late in the evening and she gently falls asleep on the swing. Alka learns from Shwetang about Nand. He patiently waits for Buddha to speak to him. He listens to his discourse on indulgence and abstinence. He does not resist being shorn but refuses to take the begging bowl. Finally, with a revulsion, he leaves for the forest. When Shwetang leaves, Alka gently swings the swing.

Nand, followed by Anand, comes. His clothes are torn and stained with blood. His head is shaved. There is an argument between Nand and Anand. Nand expresses his disgust for renunciation. Anand says that his rejection of the bowl is only a part of his answer. He adds that his answer cannot be final until peace is restored to his mind. When Anand leaves, Nand feels happy that he need not face Sundari's queries immediately. He thinks that he has not changed in any way though his appearance has changed. He says to himself, facing sleeping Sundari:

> Now that it's out, what difference does it make? Will it not grow again in a few days? There would be a difference if my heart is changed, my eyes are changed (*turns to swing and pulls at it*). In my heart there's still the same love for you. In my eyes you're still beautiful. The sandal-dot on your forehead has dried up. I am sorry about that. I shall wet it. (14)

As he wets the dot with oil on Sundari's forehead, she wakes up. Immediately, he leaps back and hides. She asks, 'Who is it?'. Alka and Shwetang come and say that nobody has come. But she insists that she has seen a stranger 'with the head of a monk and the rest of the body that of a wounded soldier.' She perceives the strange behaviour of Alka and Shwetang who have just caught a glimpse of Nand. She becomes aware of Nand the moment he moves. She does not agree with Alka who says that Nand has returned.

> SUNDARI. (*gets up*) No, he has not returned. It is someone else who has returned.
>
> NAND. (*goes up to her*) You too feel I am another person? Just because some one forcibly cut my hair? (14)

When they are alone, Nand explains why he could not return soon. Sundari tells him about her opinion of him:

> I have known that you were as common as the common people, that you could be influenced as easily as them. The only difference is that while ordinary folk may be influenced for ever, you could be influenced every time, by almost anything that has the least power to influence. (15)

He denies her opinion and attributes his behaviour to his inner conflict. He elaborates on his discovery:

> Not because of any influence . . . only out of an inner compulsion. And yesterday and today I stayed out . . . . again not because of any influence, but because of yet another need. . . . I have known for long I could't always spend my life here. . . . Nor always be cut off from here. Where how, on which point to live is a question I've never been able to answer for myself. I know you don't like to listen to all this. And you don't like it because you think you're the centre of my universe, round whom I gravitate like a planet. But I take myself to be a broken-down planet that has neither any orbit nor any centre. (15)

She asks him if there is anything for him. He says: "I am nothing. My inner needs are also illusive." (16) She feels vexed and says: "You are free to go and search for as many points as you like. Don't shut them with words." (16) She is exhausted by fury and goes down on hands and knees while he, with bowed head, goes out. His mind becomes a battlefield for life and death impulses. He himself says: "I co-existed with the instincts of self-destruction and self-preservation." (14) He represents the modern man who, caught by the inner conflict, denies life symbolised by Sundari. Rakesh says that Sundari symbolises life as a force.[10] Thus, alienated from life, the modern man suffers from existential angst.

Vivek Dutta Jha points out, "One aspect of his plays is that he pays much attention to the internal conflict in the minds of his characters."[11] This play deals with the inner conflict much more than Rakesh's other plays. The theme is contemporary though the time is chronologically two thousand and five hundred years ago. Rakesh explains this in his interview: "this is a dilemma into which each one of us is somehow split. Man is as genuine in his quest as any Buddha, and he is as genuine in his quest of pleasure as, say, any statue from Konark. So it is this dilemma of today's man that I wanted to portray in this second play."[12] Veena Noble Dass observes, that "The agony of choice is the theme and focal point of this play."[13] This can be resolved in a proper synthesis, a reunification of both the impulses rather than by choosing one.

Sircar's *Bhoma* depicts the impact of lovelessness on our society. The playwright learns about Bhoma and Sundarban from Tushar Kanjilal, the headmaster of Rangabelia Village School. Sircar, in the preface, writes about the evolution of the play:

> But Bhoma's story is not there in this play. Seeing, feeling and learning about our surroundings shock us, hurt us, anger us—these have come out in disjoined, dramatic pictures. Bhoma's picture was then part of those pieces. But when those pictures were strung together into a play then somehow it was Bhoma's image which started to become the link and at the end the play could not be called anything but Bhoma. (45)

Satabdi does the play with six actors. ONE goes on searching for Bhoma while THREE speaks of love. Bhoma is not a character yet his presence is felt throughout the play. He grows from a poor peasant into a powerful image. The play has collectively been created by Sircar and Satabdi team. It has neither characters nor a plot.

Six actors, dressed identically, mime various agricultural operations from cutting the trees to make the land arable, to harvesting and then working with machines. ONE says that he knows about Bhoma. But he cannot give any details about him since he does not know him completely. There is a discussion about the evolution:

> TWO. The blood of fish is cold.
> ONE. The blood of man is also cold. Theory of Evolution. Darwin. Had man's blood not grown cold, he wouldn't have survived.
> THREE. What would he have done then?
> ONE. Died. Become extinct, like the Dinosaurs.
> THREE. The blood of the Dinosaurs. Was it cold, or warm?
> ONE. I don't know. (47)

The argument is not scientific. But it suggests lovelessness, lack of sympathy for fellow human beings. Maybe human beings, like Dinosaurs, will become extinct if they continue to be loveless and apathetic.

TWO talks about his job, his family and his problems. THREE feels bored and shouts at him to stop talking. But he talks about his love for a girl while others laugh at him. Then, their attention shifts to tourism and cities. It leads to the urban development.

> FOUR. Television! Television! It's here now. Don't worry.
> FIVE. Metro Rail! Flyovers! The second Hooghly Bridge! Don't worry. (49)

ONE hints at the need of developing the rural area: "But seventy-five per cent of India's population live in villages, not in cities." (49) Poets described villages beautifully and governments give great publicity to the village welfare programmes:

> THREE. The village! The lovely village! The charming village! The beautiful village!
>
> FOUR. The special village welfare programmes—on the radio. (50)

Then, a dance of greed by affluent business people is acted. The dance stops abruptly as ONE calls 'Bhoma' aloud. He says to the other, "Bhoma is the forest. Bhoma is the paddy field. Bhoma is the village." (50) Peasants have to grow food grains for all the people. But they are not supplied with water, seeds and fertilizers. Most of them are so poor that they cannot afford fertilizers and water pump sets for their small lands. Consequently, they become hired labourers on the lands of rich peasants and landlords. They get four rupees a day as wages and each labourer has five to ten dependents. ONE describes their plight:

> At four rupees a day you can't afford to buy rice; wheat, yes, but not enough for chapatis. If you make a porridge of it with water and salt it goes a long way and fills you up. If you can't get wheat flour, there's cornflour, if you can't even get hold of that, you starve. You can't always get a four rupees a day job, may be at most a hundred or a hundred and twenty-five days a year. (54)

They do not get even that work in summer and they have to starve. But the urban middle class remains indifferent to the pathetic condition of the village poor. Moreover, they want more and more facilities for their city which will make villages poorer and poorer. A city demands billions of rupees for its development whereas a few million rupees is enough for the irrigation of a few thousand acres of land in villages. ONE says:

> There's no electricity but there are the poles and wires—all these three years. . . . If we get electricity, if the canals are dredged, if we have more tube wells—only 3 million rupees—then the whole of the Simulpur Anchal, all the 3000 acres of land—will yield gold! Gold! (54)

And others talk about the development of their city:

> TWO. The second bridge—only 600 million rupees.
>
> THREE. Digging in Calcutta for better streets and better sewers—

only 2000 million rupees spent so far.

FOUR. The Metro rail will cost only 3000 million rupees. (55)

This throws light on the city and village polarization and on the exploitation of millions of villages by a few cities. Ella Dutta, talking about Sircar's aim, points out: "What he wishes to communicate through his theatre are clearcut facts, concrete truths about what is happening in the villages at the grass-roots level, the nature of exploitation both industrial and agricultural, the urban stranglehold on the rural economy." (viii)

In villages, landlords exploit poor peasants while in cities, industrialists exploit craftsmen. The play illustrates this. Mahamaya Engineering Company manufactures diesel pumpsets for Samson and Blackbird Company. They stick their name plate on the set and prepare the specification literature for them. They get only two thousand five hundred rupees for each set which Samson and Blackbird Company sells for four thousand, six hundred and twenty five rupees. Mahamaya Engineering Company gets its money only after the sets are sold. They need working capital to manufacture new sets so they approach the manager of a bank for a loan. The manager refuses to sanction the loan of a few thousand rupees to them but he readily sanctions Samson and Blackbird Company a big loan of one hundred and thirty thousand without security. The poor craftsmen sell their Mahamaya Engineering Company because they cannot maintain it any more for lack of capital.

Lovelessness is hinted at again. The exploitation of ages facilitated by lovelessness is also referred to:

ONE. My heart bleeds. Can a drop of it germinate even a prickly thorn on this earth?

TWO. This earth has sucked up so much blood already, hasn't it? (58)

The intensity of exploitation is expressed very effectively by exploiting the image of blood. It is repeated in Sircar's another play in another manner: "Blood has an advantage. The rains wash away all the blood on the earth. It is washed into drains, from the drains to the rivers, from the rivers into the sea. It is not generally known that sea water has a high blood content, and the blood content is increasing day by day."[15]

Similarly, FIVE uses the word 'blood' conveying various meanings. He says, "Give me blood, I'll give you jobs," "Give me blood, I'll give you permits" (62) and "Give me blood, I'll give you a kingdom." (63) The word means 'money,' 'murder' and 'sacrifice.' But it invariably implies exploitation and oppression. Sircar invigorates the image of blood step by step. The image is finally hurled at the urban middle class to make them feel remorseful for their apathy to the rural poor peasants: "Bhoma's blood, red blood, blossoms into white jasmines of rice on our plates. Twice every day." (76) ONE again conveys this towards the end of the play:

> There's the taste of Bhoma's blood on the tongue. We drink Bhoma's blood, and laugh and play. There's blood dripping down the sides of our mouths, dripping, the poisonous trees are growing, growing. My blood, man's blood, becomes cold, c-o-l-d, c-o-l-d. (88)

The play repeatedly attempts to prove that exploitation is not only inhuman in itself but also caused by the lovelessness of man.

Lovelessness is encouraged and promoted in several ways. Fine arts are used to make people loveless and thus indifferent to the suffering of the poor.

> TWO. (*in agony*) Beggars and dogs fighting over leftovers from the wedding feast thrown out on the street.
>
> ONE. Drown that noise with Ravi Shankar's sitar. (64)

Competitiveness and individualism make people loveless and materialistic, so material things become more valuable to them than men. They forget loving in their mad scramble in this hierarchized society:

> ONE. Lots of things, lots and lots. . . . In life's walls there are many shelves and niches. There are rows and rows of fascinating objects. Look at them, mark them, choose them. (64)
>
> THREE. Is there love on those shelves, in those niches?
>
> ONE. (*very seriously*). Not on the shelves, not in the niches. (65)

Religion which usually preaches love is converted into a loveless, materialistic institution. Even God is made an agent of granting material things rather than salvation or divine love:

> ONE. Don't believe in love.
>
> THREE. Then what should we believe in?

ONE. In things. Things, things and more things.
THREE. Only things?
ONE. You can even believe in God. A God that gives you things. A God that takes away things from the unbelievers. (65)

Competitiveness and individualism strain the relations between parents and children and the lovelessness boomerangs in every family. The parents of middle-class families sell their property and borrow money to educate their children. Even the country also spends a great deal on their education. But being highly educated, they leave their parents and their country, in debts and serve abroad:

TWO. I'll sell my pots and pans, but he'll get his education.
THREE. Yes, yes, sell your pots and pans.
FOUR. Your country will also sell its pots and pans to educate him.
FIVE. Thousands and thousands of pots and pans will be spent to educate him.
SIX. Educated, he will depart in glory for America. (68)

This throws light on the fact that third world countries like India are exploited by the advanced countries like America in the same manner as villages are exploited by cities.

Individualism destroys our love of nation and breeds dishonesty and corruption. The rulers exploit their nation and deposit their money in Switzerland. So the country becomes more and more bankrupt while the rulers grow more and more affluent. They make use of the press and mass media to conceal their fake patriotism and to present themselves as noble statesmen to the people:

ONE. You'll borrow a hundred, and repay a hundred?
TWO. That's what it amounts to.
ONE. That means you'll become bankrupt then?
TWO. Bless me, it's the country that will become bankrupt, why should I? My money is in a bank in Switzerland.
ONE. Shalt thou not be called a traitor by the nation?
TWO. Who dares call me that? I'm a patriot and I'll remain one.
ONE. How?
TWO. Microphone. Newspapers. Radio Television. Above everything else the 'I' in man. (69)

The egotism in everybody, supported by lovelessness, sustains the exploitative system. In democracy, all people are provided with equal opportunities in principle. But the result is that only a few privileged people reap the fruit in practice. Consequently individual rulers become affluent while the government becomes bankrupt.

The worst consequence of lovelessness is the nuclear warfare. Nuclear weapons not only destroy millions of people but also cause deformity to millions of children at foetal stage. Several countries do nuclear tests which pollute the environment with radioactivity:

> ONE. All the experiments with atom bombs that have been conducted up to 1962 on this earth. . . .
>
> TWO. FOUR, FIVE, SIX. The earth . . .
>
> ONE. Have released enough radioactivity to cause the birth of the million maimed and deformed children. . . . (71-72)

ONE later talks about how long radioactivity lasts: "Twenty-four thousand years! Human civilization is only five thousand years old. Within this time man has made arrangements for the next twenty-four thosuand years." (73) Yet people do not realize the colossal lethal power of nuclear weapons and feel very happy about their country's becoming a nuclear power:

> TWO, FOUR, SIX. Rejoice! Rejoice!
> ONE. India becomes a nuclear power!
> TWO, FOUR, SIX, Rejoice! Rejoice!
> ONE. Number six in the world! (72)

THREE explains ONE how nuclear power can be used for peaceful purposes. But ONE deflates the complacency: "Peace. Peaceful birth, Peaceful death. In between the two—a peaceful, deformed life." (72) Thus, lovelessness is behind all kinds of violent conflicts from family feud leading to a murder, to a world war causing a colossal carnage.

Sircar attempts to explore the causes and effects of lovelessness and find out the solution to the problem:

> TWO. There's no Bhoma. There's only I. (*Take a start.*)
> *The race starts. Everyone tries to push the other aside and go ahead.*
> THREE. No, no, its I. (*Tries to overtake* ONE)
> FOUR. Not you, it's I.
> FIVE. Oh no, it's I.
> SIX. Stop, stop, it's I.

They are all racing now
ALL. I, I, I, I, I. (66)

Sircar is able to say through his play what Steiner says through psychology. He shows here clearly how competition and individualism cause lovelessness. The antidote to this is collectivism and cooperation.

ONE. *(over their voice)* I, I, I, I—and a little more security. I, I, I, I, and a little ease. I, I, I, I, and a little luxury. Bhoma, you, I, they, when will it all become a great 'we,' can you tell me, Bhoma? (66-67)

The solution is the dissolution of all egos into a great unified 'we.' But it is generally presumed that competition increases productivity. Steiner observes: ". . .competition between people brings about increased productivity, the major benefit of which is reaped by a privileged few with enough given back to people to keep them competing." (323) Sircar drives home this fact in a different way:

TWO. To every single 'I' I shall show the way to a Swiss bank.
ONE. How many I's will reach a Swiss bank?
TWO. One or two. One in ten million. So What? This is called ambition. This is called 'being established.' (69-70)

Sircar exposes the lovelessness of society which facilitates the oppression and exploitation of peasants, workers, villages and developing countries by landlords, industrialists, cities and advanced countries in this play. But many critics focus their study on oppression and exploitation. K. Venkateswarlu comments: "Thus, *Bhoma* presents a vivid picture of the oppressed peasant by dramatizing a series of scenes in which he is socially oppressed and economically exploited."[16] Shampa Bhattacharjee points out: "Through a series of concretes borrowed from this social scenery, Sircar, in *Bhoma*, harshly exposes the spirits of the oppressed rural population against the backdrop of the 'grandeur' of the city of Calcutta."[17] Of course, these critics do take note of Sircar's indictment of the apathy of the middle class towards the poor peasant. Veena Noble Dass observes: "When Sircar came in contact with the villagers of the Sundarbans, he was shocked by the dehumanized condition of their life. But more than shocked he was enraged by the fact that the urban community of West Bengal could be so totally indifferent to the impoverishment of the villagers in the Sundarbans." (73) The indifference is due to lovelessness. People are not only indifferent to the suffering of the poor but also loveless to one another:

ONE. My heart has dried up. My heart is a piece of leather. Can you spare me a drop of water to moisten it?
TWO. Sorry, go on. (74)

Everybody needs and wants love but nobody is ready to love others. T.S. Eliot depicts this spiritual steritity in his *Waste Land*. In this, water symbolizes love and compassion:

Here is no water but only rock
Rock and no water and the sandy road.[18]

Sircar does not seem to believe in Marxian model of class struggle. He does not attribute this human misery to the exploiting class though he does criticise exploiting landlords and capitalists and oppressive rulers. He points out the collective responsiblity of all men and women. So he calls every human being a culprit in his play, *There's No End*.

THE MAN. (*Shouts*) What is all this? Everything is going topsy-turvy. Who is the accused? Who is the witnes? The jury? The judge? Everything is mixed up.
SUMANTA. There is no accused. I am the accused. You are the accused. You, you, you—all of you are the accused—We are all the accused![19]

All the characters, including industrialists, artists, professors, workers and beggars, are found guilty. They all say: "There's no end—the trial will go on forever."[20] Every human being, like King Oedipus,[21] is the culprit, the victim and the judge. Sircar conveys this idea in *Bhoma* clearly and emphatically:

THREE. No, this cannot be! This cannot happen! We won't let this happen!
ONE. Who will not let it happen?
THREE. Man! Man has created all this. Man is going to stop it.
ONE. With what?
THREE. With love! Man still loves man, doesn't he? Tell me! Doesn't he love?
ONE. (*Slowly*) Man loves. He still loves.
THREE. Then?

ONE. But the blood of man is getting cold. I don't know how long man will be able to love.

THREE. Is there no way out then? No way at all? To keep the blood warm? To bring back love? To change the world?

ONE. (*almost to himself*) Bhoma. (76)

Thus, Bhoma becomes a powerful symbol as the play progresses. He is not just a poor peasant. Bhoma is the jungle. Bhoma is the cornfield. Bhoma is the village. (76) He also symbolises love, compassion and humanity. The oppression of Bhoma has caused all the problems and the freedom of Bhoma solves all the problems.

Sircar believes in the credo, 'From everybody according to his ability, to everybody according to his needs.'[22] He shows how such an egalitarian society, obviates all oppression and exploitation:

ONE. This earth belongs to ALL of us, doesn't it, Bhoma? If we ALL of us, could work our hardest to make everything we need and then ALL of us shared all we produced, then that queer picture that lets us buy up your blood to drink, the picture that you don't have and therefore can't get your rice—if we could destroy for ever that queer, obscene picture—I can't explain it, Bhoma! I can only understand—if you don't rise up with your axe, then the forest of poisonous trees will never be cleared! (86)

The image of poisonous trees is usually understood to refer to the class of exploiters and oppressors. K. Sumana, for example, observes: "The society full of opportunists and exploiters is presented as a forest of poisonous trees and Bhoma, an aboriginal barbarian as a woodcutter. Bhoma is an archetype of the oppressed exploited peasant who, at long last, takes up his 'rusty axe,' grinds and sharpens it to cut the poisonous trees that grow around him."[23] Actually, whether a person becomes an exploiter or a worker is determined not by biological factors such as genes, but by socio-cultural environment. So until and unless such oppressive and exploitative socio-cultural environment is exterminated, exploiters and oppressors will continue to exist even if they are annihilated physically. The history of China, Russia and other socialist countries and the revolutionary movements even in India prove this. And Sircar's interpretation rejects the concept of dictatorship of the proletariat as the fountainhead of totalitarian tyranny as Gowri Ramnarayan points out. (75) So the image of the forest of poisonous trees must refer to the system, the socio-cultural environment rather than individuals. *Bhoma* emphasizes the need of love and compassion to better our society.

Pramila Devi explores the theme of violence in Tendulkar's plays in her dissertation "The Theatre of Violence."[24] Many critics think that Tendulkar's plays deal with violence in its various forms. But Tendulkar contradicts them: "Even in plays like *Sakharam Binder* and *Vultures*, the theme is not violence. Violence comes as a way of life—a natural way of life if you consider the background of the characters. It is there as part of the functioning of a character."[25] Kumar Ketkar complains that Tendulkar "began to fondle the theme of violence mindlessly."[26] And Sudhir Sonalkar critically comments, "Tendulkar's violence shocks and even when it disturbs, the ethical question remains both untouched and unanswered."[27] Tendulkar portrays the ruthless violence that we find in our society. His play, *The Vultures*, depicts violence in an upper middle class family. Competitiveness, individualism and their sequel, lovelessness have attacked the family finally and strained human relations within the family. When material things become more important than man, loveless people will resort to any gross atrocity. As Tendulkar feels, violence becomes a natural consequence of such a situation. A. Jaganmohan Chari and E. Renuka point out, "This play enacts the goriest of the family relations existing in our society today."[28]

Hari Pitale cheats Sakharam, his own brother, in business and prospers. His sons, Ramakant and Umakant, and his daughter Manik inherit his culture of loveless individualism. They all form a family of vultures. Ramakant, Umakant and Manik, like their father, are ever ready to cheat one another to get more money and they do not hesitate to kill one another to get a great share of the property. Manik therefore becomes paranoid. She says to Rama, her sister-in-law: "So I should leave it [the door] open, should I? So you can come and strangle me, all of you? It's because I take care that I've survived in this house!"[29] Hari Pitale himself talks about his children's character:

> If I die, it'll be a release! They're all waiting for it. But I'm your own father, after all! If I die, I'll become a ghost. I'll sit on your chest! I won't let you enjoy a rupee of it. I earned it all. Now, these wolves, these bullies! (209)

Among these wolves and vultures, live two innocent lambs: Rajaninath, the illegimate son of Hari Pitale and Rama, the wife of Ramakant. Rajaninath like a chorus comments on the characters and incidents through his poems. For instance, he writes about Rama:

Then she stepped over
The bridal measure,
And crossed the threshold of her new home.
But it was no home.
Not a home, but a hole in a tree
Where Vultures lived
In the shape of men.
A haunted burning-ground surrounded by evil ghosts.
Was that a home? (204)

Ramakant does not want to pay his servants properly. He and his brother hate each other and they both hate Manik, their own sister. And all the three hate their father. They prefer money to a man. Only Rama and Rajaninath have love and compassion.

One day, Ramakant, Umakant and Manik learn that their father has got a large sum of money in a bank. So, they become united and pay fake reverence to their father. He feels happy because his sons have successfully sent his brother out. But they soon start fighting and hurt their father deliberately in their fake fight. They create such a panic that he begs them not to kill him. Finally, he yields and writes a cheque. They get the cash and spend it on liquor. These loveless people seek pleasure in liquor and violence.

Ramakant and Umakant exhaust their share of money and want some more. So, they decide to blackmail the Raja of Hondur who is in love with Manik. They want to prevent her from informing her lover about their blackmailing him. Therefore, Ramakant suggests that they should break her leg for this. So, they successfully break the leg of their own sister. They hope to get twenty thousand rupees from the Raja of Hondur by blackmailing him. Later, they learn that the Raja has died of heart attack. They feel greatly frustrated and fail to contain their frustration. Ramakant says to Umakant: "The Raja's alive. In little Manik's belly. The bloody bastard, damn him! Bloody enemy! The traitor! I'll shoot him, brother." (247) And later, he adds, 'Let's abort him!' So, Ramakant kicks Manik very hard on the belly while Umakant holds her fast. Thus, they cause abortion.

Ramakant takes his wife to doctors and saints because she cannot bear him any children. She is vexed with visiting doctors and saints very frequently. She knows that the fault is with her husband who has become impotent on account of drinking liquor excessively. She says to Rajaninath: "It's not the fault of doctors, of learned men, of saints and sages! It's not even my fault! This womb's healthy and sound, I swear it! I was born to become a mother. This soil's rich, it's hungry. But the seed won't take root." (241) She adds that her suffering is an endless *Sati*. She, therefore, prefers death to the hell of her sterile wifehood. Rajaninath understands her agony and takes her into his arms. She feels secure and happy in his embrace. She enjoys his love and he makes her pregnant. Arundhati Banerjee in her Introduction to *Five plays* throws light on the aspect of love between Rama and Rajaninath, "The sexual aspect of their association is merely an extension of their love which is the only redeeming feature in the morbid and claustrophobic atmosphere of the family." (xii- xiii)

Rama feels claustrophobic and says to her husband, "This house is devouring me." (249) She begs him to be with her. But he insists that he should leave to look after his business. She, finally, implores him in anguish:

> Take a job somewhere! Whatever you get. Never mind if it doesn't pay well. We'll live in poverty, if we have to. You, me, our baby. The three of us. We'll make a feast of crumbs. We'll eat once a day. We'll endure whatever we have to. I'll slave as hard as you want. Gladly. But let's finish this death by imprisonment. Let's end this dreadful play-acting. Stop this murderous deceit. Honestly! Put an end to it. Let's get out of this overpowering house. Go far away. No one, no one at all can live happily here. Not at all . . . never at all. (250-51)

She intuitively knows that the aura of the house is full of individualism, competitiveness and power games. Such a house cannot accommodate love, compassion and joy. It is a real hell. Ramakant who is intoxicated by egoism and male chauvinism cannot perceive the wisdom of his wife's advice; nor can he understand her agony. So, he says to her: "Look here, Rama! In this house, we're not accustomed to listening to any smartness from woman! No man in our family's been a bloody henpecked husband, What? I know very well indeed what to do, what not to do. No need for a woman to teach me sense." (251) Then, he goes away. Rama also fears the dire consequence of the revealing of the truth about her pregnancy. But she cannot help it.

Ramakant and Umakant discuss sharing the business and property. Umakant learns that there is a double mortgage on their house. Ramakant advises his brother to go ahead with his flourishing business and leave the house to him. But Umakant demands him to settle their account about their father's hidden property, their sister's money and mother's jewels. Otherwise, he will not leave the house. Then, he tells his brother that his wife is carrying in her womb the child of Rajaninath.

This enrages Ramakant, and he scolds Umakant and twists his hand. So, Umakant goes out. Ramakant calls Rama down and talks to her tenderly only to elicit her tender feelings for Rajaninath. He succeeds in his attempt and suspects that his wife has committed adultery. Later, he in his rage causes abortion to his wife.

Hari Pitale realizes that his legitimate children will kill him for property. He knows that Rajaninath, his illegitimate son, is humane. So, he seeks his protection from his own children and promises Rajaninath to make his will in his favour by backdating it. He says:

> I *am* telling you. I can't endure this, Rajani. Nor would you. This must be changed. Not by anyone else. By us. Listen to what I'm telling you. I'm behind you. If you want, I'll raise the money. I've got some credit still. I've made a new will. A backdated one. I've got hold of a lawyer for the seal, too. In this will, I've divided the whole estate between you and Manik. (259)

Rajaninath is repulsed by the property as it has made the people loveless vultures. He detests the very idea of inheriting the property. So he cannot show any compassion to him and mercilessly asks him to get out. At the end of the play, he expresses his hidden compassion for the loveless vultures in the family though they have ill-treated him:

> The tale of the five vultures
> Had this end.
> The story of men accursed.
> Or else of vultures cursed
> To live their lives as men.
> Oh, show them some compassion! (265)

Rajaninath fructifies the womb of Rama while Ramakant aborts it. Thus, in the play, they symbolise love and lovelessness respectively. Veena Noble Dass points out, "Tendulkar has made use of joint family system, but he goes to the extent of demolishing this system in the family of Pitales, where each character is responsible for the breakdown of the system." (94) The demolition of the family is indeed due to lovelessness and individualism.

To conclude, Mohan Rakesh probes into the internal conflict of the human mind that leads to lovelessness. He shows in *The Great Swans of the Waves* how the conflict between the love and the renunciation of life causes spiritual ailment, and how the extremity of renunciation leads to lovelessness. Badal Sircar in *Bhoma* explores the sociological implications of lovelessness. He illustrates how competition and individualism lead to lovelessness and how lovelessness makes possible the inhuman exploitation of peasants, workers, villages and developing countries by landlords, capitalists, cities and advanced countries. Vijay Tendulkar's *The Vultures* throws light on the impairment of human relations even within the family caused by lovelessness. It elucidates how lovelessness can bring about most inhuman violence even within a family. Thus, gender inequality, social inequality, power games and the cultural oppression of spontaneity, intuition and rationality sustain lovelessness.

NOTES

1. "Where is the tradition?," Interview, *Frontline*, September 25, 1992, 75.
2. *The Anatomy of Human Destructiveness* (New York: Fawcett Crest, 1975) 25.
3. See *Shiva Purana* any version by any publisher.
4. (London: Routledge, 1959).
5. Bhagwan Shree Rajneesh, *Get out of Your Own Way* (Poona: Rajneesh Foudation, 1977) 135.
6. *Scripts People Live* (New York: Bantam Books, 1980) 139-40.
7. Mohan Rakesh, *The Great Swans of the Waves*, trans. Paul Jacob and Meena Williams, *Enact*, Jan.-Feb. 1973, 1.
8. Mohan Rakesh "*Lehron Ke Rajhans:* Preface to the Revised Edition," *Enact*, Jan.-Feb. 1973, no page.
9. "Rakesh, the Playwright" *Enact*, Jan-Feb., 1973, no page.
10. Mohan Rakesh, Interview, *Enact*, May 1971, no page.
11. Vivek Dutta Jha, 'Mohan Rakesh and his Plays,' *Enact*, Jan.-Feb. 1973, no page.
12. Mohan Rakesh, Interview, *A Journal of South Asian Literature*, IX, 2-3 (1973), 33.
13. Veena Noble Dass, *Modern Indian Drama in English Translation* (New Delhi: n.p, 1988) 17.
14. Badal Sircar, *Bhoma*, trans. Badal Sircar and Kalyani Ghose *Three Plays* (Calcutta: Seagull Books, 1985).
15. *Stale News*, trans. Samik Bandyopadhyay, *Three Plays* (Calcutta: Seagull, 1985) 133.
16. "Badal Sircar's Third Theatre," S.K. University, 1993, 56.
17. "Badal Sircar's Street Plays: A Thematic Study," Kakatiya University, 1994, 280.
18. *The Faber Book of Modern Verse*, ed. Michael Roberts (London: Faber, 1965) 101.
19. Badal Sircar, *There's No End*, trans. K. Raha, *Enact* (19).

20. Sircar, 19.
21. See Sophocles, *King Oedipus*, *The Theban Plays,* trans E.F. Walting (Harmondsworth: Penguin, 1974).
22. Qtd. Gowri Ramnarayan, "The Endless Road of Badal Sircar's Free Theatre," *Frontline,* 28 Aug. 1992, 75.
23. "The Importance of Indian Street Theatre with special reference to the Plays of Badal Sircar," *Indian Literature Today*, ed. R.K. Dhawan (Delhi: Prestige, 1994) vol. I, p. 65.
24. "The Theatre of Violence: A Study of Vijay Tendulkar's Plays," S.K. University, 1993.
25. Vijay Tendulkar, "Interview," *The Indian Express*, 27 March 1983, Magazine section, 5.
26. "Tendulkar's Human Zoo," *The Illustrated Weekly of India*, 20 Nov. 1983, 24.
27. "Vijay Tendulkar and the Metaphor of Violence," *The Illustrated Weekly of India*, Nov. 20, 1983, 21.
28. "The Plays of Vijay Tendulkar," *New Quest*, Jan.-Feb. 1988, 29.
29. Vijay Tendulkar, *The Vultures*, trans. Priya Adarkar, *Five Plays* (Bombay: Oxford UP, 1992) 207.

Conclusion

> Man lives with illusions because these illusions make the misery of real life bearable that is to say, if he can wake up from the half-dream state, then he can come to his senses, become aware of his proper forces and powers, and change reality in such a way that illusions are no longer necessary.
>
> Erich Fromm

In the beginning, human beings lived naturally and never faced the problems of the civilized men and women. As they gradually grew conscious of their identity, they were alienated from Nature and they began to realize their biological inadequacies. They have constructed this world of culture and civilization to compensate for their inadequacies and to overcome their feelings of inferiority. Culture and civilization have suppressed their real nature and distorted their personality. Consequently, they have become fragmented, deformed and dehumanized.

Human beings are born whole and healthy. Yet each human being becomes fragmented, deformed and dehumanized as he or she grows up in the cultural environment. It may be said to operate in six ways and cause six cultural deformities—gender, social, political, physical, mental and spiritual. All these support and sustain one another and form a resilient network, a labyrinth where men and women get lost. Modern Indian Drama in English, as represented by Mohan Rakesh, Girish Karnad, Vijay Tendulkar and Badal Sircar, seems to reflect all these cultural deformities of Indian society.

Gender deformity seems to have preceded the other cultural deformities. Human beings are originally neither masculine nor feminine, but cultural attributes go to make men masculine and women feminine. Consequently, in men, the faculties of controlling, rationality and adaptability develop while those of nurturing and intuition are suppressed. Similarly, in women, the faculties of nurturing, intuition and adaptability develop while those of controlling and rationality are suppressed. These acquired, incomplete and deformed personalities help men and women perform the functions culturally attributed to them and disable them to take up other tasks. And women suffer more than men on account of gender deformity as our society is patriarchal.

Gender deformity is comprehensively illustrated in Tendulkar's *Kamala*. Jaisingh, whose faculties of rationality and leadership enable him to be a successful journalist, collect sensational news for his paper. His faculties of nurturing and intuition remain underdeveloped and so he cannot realize that he exploits women while he tries to expose their exploitation and oppression by big men. Sarita, his wife, looks after all his needs at home effectively as her faculties of nurturing and intuition help her in this. As she is educated, she becomes a sophisticated wife. She is under the illusion that she is free. She realizes that she is also a slave as Kamala, the tribal woman, triggers her awareness with an innocent question. Jaisingh loses his job for exposing the flesh trade. Thus, the play shows that women are slaves at home while men are slaves at work.

Karnad's *Naga-Mandala* questions the gender-biased justice which favours men. Appanna treats Rani, his wife, contemptuously. He lives with his concubine and ignores Rani. Naga, a Cobra, assumes Appanna's form and makes love to Rani at night. Thus, Rani commits adultery without knowing it whereas Appanna does the same thing openly and unashamedly. Yet the Village Elders ask only Rani to take an ordeal to prove her innocence. Tendulkar's *Silence! The Court is in Session* also challenges patriarchal value system. The fellow actors accuse Benare of fornication and torture her mentally in the name of a mock-trial while Prof. Damle, the male culprit, who exploited the young lady sexually, is not found fault with. In Rakesh's *Half-Way House*, Savitri feels greatly frustrated as her husband does not fit her culturally acquired concept of a masculine man. She makes her life miserable and creates a hell for others.

Social deformity brings about inequality though human beings are born equal. The divisions of men and women into various castes and classes and their hierarchy are culturally programmed and transmitted from one generation to another. The people of higher rungs exploit and oppress those of lower rungs in our hierarchized society. The boundaries of caste are strongly guarded to sustain the social deformity in Indian society. The caste system has survived several revolutions and reforms by great leaders like Basavanna.

Karnad's *Tale-Danda* is a dramatization of Basavanna's movement against the caste system eight hundred years ago. Several people from various places come to Kalyan and join Basavanna's ideal movement. They shed caste and become *sharanas*. They work hard and take what is enough for their sustenance. They forget their differences and dine together. All this does not provoke any active opposition. Then *sharanas* perform a marriage between a dalit boy and a Brahmin girl. This leads to a violent battle between them and orthodox people. After the carnage of *sharanas* and the ravage of their property by the royal army, several *sharanas* flee into the forest. After a few centuries, they emerge as a new caste. This throws light on the resilience of social deformity.

Sircar's *Stale News* exposes the severity of social deformity in India. The dramatist juxtaposes the instances of gross exploitation and oppression of the British India and those of the post-colonial India. He also shows how the government oppresses the people of lower strata of the society to protect those of higher strata. The idea of man's baseness is ironically highlighted by repeating the statement that Man is the greatest creature on Earth. In Rakesh's *One Day in Ashadha*, Kalidasa, in his scramble to the higher rung in society, marries the princess after he becomes the poet laureate in Ujjain. Thus he betrays his love, Mallika who has inspired great poetry in him. All these plays prove that social deformity makes people inhuman.

If political deformity is not there, all human beings are equally powerful. They have enough power to help themselves and change their way of life for better. The people of lower rungs in this hierarchized society give away their immense power to those of higher rungs by taking the hierarchy for granted. The imbalance of power brings about power games. A power game involves three major roles: Rescuer, Persecutor and Victim. The Rescuer feels guilty about his superiority if he cannot make use of it in rescuing the Victim without being asked. The Persecutor feels angry at the inferiority of the Victim and seeks to reform him or her through punishment. The Victim allows himself or herself to be rescued or persecuted. These roles form a triangle called Drama Triangle as expounded by Karpman. People usually have one favourite role each, yet they shift to other roles. The power game may involve two minor roles: Stage-Manager and Spectator.

Karnad's *Tughlaq* illustrates Karpman Drama Triangle. In the play, Muhammad plays the Rescuer. He believes that he can alone save his people. So, he gets his own father and brother killed and becomes the king. He introduces several reforms to build an ideal kingdom. All his reforms are exploited by people like Aziz. Then, he goes down to the role of Victim. He does not tolerate any obstacle in his path and assassinates several people who oppose his idealism. Thus, he shifts to the role of Persecutor. Soon after, he returns to his favourite role—the Rescuer. This shifting of roles can be found in other roles. The play shows that playing the Rescuer does not solve problems.

Tendulkar's *Ghasiram Kotwal* presents the minor roles in addition to the major ones. Ghasiram plays the Persecutor. In the beginning, he is humiliated by the people of Poona and decides to avenge it on them. He, therefore, sacrifices his daughter to the lust of Nana and becomes the Kotwal of Poona. He tortures and punishes people severely even for petty crimes. Finally the people get the permission of Nana and humiliate and kill Ghasiram. Nana plays the Stage-Manager and Peshwa, the Spectator. Sircar's *That Other History* first shows the power game in a family and finally locates the demon, the Persecutor in human mind itself. It then deplicts how that internal demon is responsible for war, violence and destruction, the dark side of history.

Physical deformity evolves as division, hierarchization and alienation invade the human body. The head (mind) and the body are divided and alienated. The head is considered the supreme organ. It carries the cultural deformity in itself. It governs the body and suppresses its sensations. Consequently, people find their lives joyless and meaningless in addition to acquiring bodily deformities depending on their occupation. So, they seek to get pleasure through alcohol and drugs and to find meaning for life in religious or secular ideals.

Karnad's *Hayavadana* exemplifies the alienation of the mind and the body and also external deformity. The play begins with the worship of Lord Ganesha, the elephant-headed god. Then, Hayavadana, the horse-headed man, is introduced. Later, he becomes a complete horse instead of a complete man as Goddess Kali grants his wish to become complete. In the main plot, Devadatta, a Brahmin, has a brilliant mind and a weak body whereas his friend, Kapila, a Shudra, has a dull mind and a strong body. Padmini, the wife of Devadatta, seeks to get a complete man. When the two friends behead themselves at the altar of Goddess Kali, she transposes their heads. Consequently, Devadatta gets Kapila's strong body while Kapila gets Devadatta's weak body. But, Devadatta loses the vigour of Kapila's body gradually as he discontinues his physical exercise in order to pursue his profession. Thus, the play conveys that the head that carries culture in itself triumphs over the body.

In Tendulkar's *Sakharam Binder*, Sakharam and Champa drink liquor and indulge in mechanical sex to overcome their joylessness whereas Lakshmi seeks to find pleasure in and meaning for her life in religious rituals. And Champa's husband gets sadistic pleasure in torturing his wife horribly and later masochistic pleasure in drinking liquor and inflicting pain on himself. In Sircar's *Evam Indrajit*, the eponymous character vainly tries to find meaning for his life in being different from common people. In his another play, *There's No End*, the central character goes on changing his course of life to make his life meaningful.

If mental deformity is not programmed, all human beings are equally capable of perceiving and understanding the world. Their mind has two faculties—rationality and intuition. These are divided and alienated. So, they do not function harmoniously and this impairs the awareness of people. Rationality is discouraged or suppressed in women and workers whereas intuition is discouraged or suppressed in educated men. And rationality is considered superior to intuition. All this is achieved through religion, education and mass media, by discounting the rationality and intuition of people and by lying. This mental deformity sustains other cultural deformities.

Sircar's *Procession* presents various situations where people are made and kept mindless. Procession is one of the rituals that religions, political parties and trade unions observe. It attracts people with its colours and sounds and makes them mindless. So, the Old Man repeatedly says: "I'm lost." Khoka who symbolizes truth is killed again and again. But, the Officer says that everything is all right and forcibly sends the people away. The Master offers the people religion when they complain about their suffering. Later, he gives them liquor when their suffering becomes too severe to be numbed by religion. Finally, he advises the Officer to drown the sorrows of the people in popular entertainment through fine arts. Thus, the awareness of the people is maimed through religious and political rituals, alcohol and other narcotic drugs and popular entertainment.

Tendulkar's *Encounter in Umbugland* exposes the role of the government and the press in making people ignorant. They arouse emotions in the people and paralyse their faculty of thinking and rationality. The Cabinet Ministers drive crowds of people against Vijaya, the Princess who tactically turns them against the Ministers themselves. The play shows how the political leaders manipulate the mindless people to strengthen their power. Sircar's play, *Scandal in Fairyland* throws light on the role of the press in the manipulation of the consciousness of the people. In Tendulkar's *Kanyadan*, Arun mindlessly persecutes Jyoti in order to feel powerful while Nath and Jyoti mindlessly rescue him in order to overcome their feelings of guilt for being Brahmins. Rakesh's *Mad Delight* depicts the fragmented mind of the modern man.

In spiritual deformity, division and alienation enter the innermost core of human personality. Life and death impulses are divided and alienated. This leads to the inner conflict between the love of life and its renunciation. This results in lovelessness. Other deformities also contribute to lovelessness. In the mad scramble to the top in the hierarchized society, people become dehumanized and this suppresses their capability to love themselves and others. This spiritual deformity facilitates ruthless exploitation and oppression and destroys human relations even within the family.

Rakesh's *The Greet Swans of the Waves* symbolically portrays the inner conflict of human soul. Nand, the protagonist, is caught in this conflict—on the one hand, he loves Sundari who symbolizes the love of life and on the other, he reveres Buddha who stands for the renunciation of life. Like the modern man, he can neither love life nor renounce it completely. The great swans on the waves represent his wavering mind.

Sircar's *Bhoma* exposes the relentless exploitation and oppression of women, peasants, workers, villages and developing countries by men, landlords, capitalists, cities and advanced countries respectively. This is attributed to lovelessness. It is repeatedly said in the play that the blood of man is cold. Then, it is conveyed that love alone can remedy the situation. Tendulkar's *The Vultures* illustrates how exploitative culture makes people vultures. Hari Pitale cheats his own brother in business. His own children use violence to extract money from him. Ramakant and Umakant break the leg of Manik, their own sister, to prevent her from informing her lover of their blackmailing him for money.

Thus, Indian Drama, as represented by Mohan Rakesh, Vijay Tendulkar, Girish Karnad and Badal Sircar, reflects the cultural deformity of Indian society in all its six aspects. Each playwright deals with each aspect of the cultural deformity from his own point of view. All the playwrights have successfully shown the severity of the problems of human mind, individual, family and society. All the playwrights have been influenced by modern and progressive thoughts and ideologies, but nobody has dogmatically followed any ideology.

In his plays, Mohan Rakesh deals with cultural deformity as reflected in the human mind. Vivek Dutta Jha rightly points out: "One aspect of his plays is that he [Rakesh] pays much attention to the internal conflict in the minds of his characters."[1] Though Mohan Rakesh focuses on human mind, other details do not suffer in his plays. He deals with gender deformity in *Half-Way House*, social deformity in *One Day in Ashadha*, mental deformity in *Mad Delight* and spiritual deformity in *The Great Swans of the Waves*. He treats physical deformtiy in his short plays, *Perhaps* and *Hunh*. But he does not touch upon political deformity in any play exclusively. He presents problems in his plays but he does not give any solutions to them. He expects the spectator or reader to search for solutions. In an interview, he says to Rajinder Paul:

> You probably attribute a much greater personality to the artist than there is in him. Mostly the artist acting as a visionary, like our great Tulsidas, has only propagated certain maxims which through tradition has come to be accepted as values of life. I cannot take up the role of a futurist as the circumstances beyond my time will not be a part of my experience. The failings of even men like Marx, the greatest visionary of our time, are quite evident. I really cannot go beyond the point of my direct confrontation of life. At that stage I go behind the wings and leave the man in the auditorium to deal with the situation as he likes.[2]

His plays elucidate the suffering of men and women, especially at psychological level, as they fall victims of socio-economic hierarchy and cultural hegemony.

Karnad deals with gender deformity in *Naga-Mandala*, social deformity in *Tale-Danda*, political deformity in *Tughlaq* and physical deformity in *Hayavadana*. He depicts the failure of solutions in his plays. His protagonists strive hard and sacrifice everything to solve the problems. But their solutions fail miserably on account of the powerful antagonism of cultural hegemony. The focus is on the individual who is protrayed as the victim of cultural deformity. Kurudavva tries to bring about harmony between Rani and Appanna with the aphrodisiac root in *Naga-Mandala*. Basavanna strives to effect harmony among the people by eradicating the caste-system in *Tale-Danda*. Muhammad endeavours hard to achieve harmony between Hindus and Muslims by effecting various reforms in *Tughlaq*. Padmini attempts to attain harmony between the mind and the body in *Hayavadana*. All the individuals fail utterly as all the deformities are socio-culturally programmed.

Tendulkar successfully brings out the ugly cultural deformity of our society through his plays. He depicts gender deformity in *Kamala*, political deformity in *Ghasiram Kotwal*, physical deformity in *Sakharam Binder*, mental deformity in *Encounter in Umbugland* and *Kanyadan* and spiritual deformity in *The Vultures*. He does not touch upon social deformity exclusively in any of his plays. He shows cultural deformity in the family and the society. In his plays we find people using violence to get pleasure, money and power. And we also see them using sex, money and violence to attain power. Tendulkar touches on the theme of power and violence in all his plays in various ways. He covers all aspects of gender deformity in his plays. He feels that the human situation is so complex that we can hardly suggest any viable solutions. He says, "I try to take my audience with me in this exploration. At its best, it can provide insights into the great jigsaw puzzle of human existence and enrich your understanding of life around you."[3] That is why he never attempts any solutions in his plays.

Sircar does not deal with women's problems exclusively. Yet he says: "I believe in equal rights for man and woman and daily watch the exploitation of woman in home and at work."[4] His feministic sympathy finds passing reference in his plays. In *Stale News*, THREE says: "Offices are closed on Sundays, half days on Saturdays. But there's no holiday for me. I had to light up the oven at daybreak and I've been on my feet ever since." (100) Sircar exposes, social deformity in *Stale News*, political deformity in *That Other History*, physical deformity in *Evam Indrajit*, mental deformity in *Procession* and spiritual deformity in *Bhoma*. His concept of the society without any cultural deformity finds illustration in his play *Beyond the Land of Hattamala*. Gowri Ramnarayan summarizes Sircar's ideas and plays in a few words: "Sircar's credo is simple: 'From everybody according to his ability, to everybody according to his needs.' When his plays began to exemplify this, even Marxists denounced him as a Utopian dreamer."[5] Sircar believes in collectivism that finds expression in his plays.

If Girish Karnad borrows his themes from myth and history and his techniques from classical and folk theatre, Mohan Rakesh and Vijay Tendulkar rely for their themes on contemporary life and history. Girish Karnad deals with all the deformities at individual, familial and societal levels in his plays though mental and spiritual deformities do not find exclusive illustration. Mohan Rakesh focuses on the inner conflict of human mind brought about by cultural deformity. The themes of power and violence find expression in Tendulkar's plays. All the deformities are illustrated in his plays though social deformity is not treated exclusively in any of his plays in English translation. All the deformities except gender deformity are elucidated in Sircar's plays. The plays of his Third Theatre depict cultural deformity at societal level. Rakesh and Tendulkar present problems in their plays and leave the task of finding out solutions to the audience whereas Karnad shows in his plays how the conventional solutions fail. However, Sircar conveys through his plays that all the people who are collectively responsible for this cultural morbidity should collectively understand the situation and find out the real solution. All the plays of these playwrights make good theatre as they have successfully blended their themes and techniques though some plays impress us more than others, depending on our sensibility.

NOTES

1. "Mohan Rakesh and his Plays," *Enact* Jan.-Feb. 1973, no page.
2. Rajinder Paul, "Mohan Rakesh Interviewed," *Enact*, May 1971, no page.
3. Vijay Tendulkar, *The Indian Express*, 5.
4. Qtd. Kavita Nagpal, "The Badal Sircar Magic," *The Hindustan Times*, April 5, 1992, 13.
5. "The Endless Road of Badal Sircar's Free Theatre," *Frontline,* 28 Aug. 1992, 75.

Bibliography

PRIMARY SOURCES

Karnad, Girish. *Tughlaq*. Delhi. Oxford UP, 1987.

______. *Hayavadana*. Delhi. Oxford UP, 1988.

______. *Naga-Mandala*. Delhi. Oxford UP, 1990.

______. *Tale-Danda*. Delhi. Ravi Dayal, 1993.

Rakesh, Mohan. *One Day in Ashadha*. Trans. Sarah K. Ensley. *Enact*, 32-33 (1969).

______. *Mad Delight*. *Enact*, 42 (1970).

______. *Half-Way House*. Trans. Bindu Batra. *Enact*, 53 (1971).

______. *The Great Swans of the Waves*. Trans. Paul Jacob and Meena Williams. *Enact*, 73-74 (1973).

______. *Short Plays*. Trans. Bindu Batra. *Enact,* 56-57 (1971).

Sircar, Badal. *Marital*. Trans. K. Raha. *Enact*, 45-55 (1970).

______. *There's No End*. Trans. K.Raha. *Enact,* 59 (1971).

______. *Evam Indrajit*. Trans. Girish Karnad. Calcutta: Oxford UP, 1974.

______. *That Other History*. Trans. Vinod L. Doshi. *Enact,* 165-66 (1980).

______. *Procession*. Trans. Samik Bandyopadhyay. *Bhoma*. Trans. Badal Sircar and Kalyani Ghose. *Stale News*. Trans. Samik Bandyopadhyay, *Three Plays*. Calcutta: Seagull, 1985.

______. *Beyond the Land of Hattamala* and *Scandal in Fairyland*. Trans. Suchanda Sarkar. Calcutta: Seagull, 1992.

Tendulkar, Vijay. *Ghasiram Kotwal*. Trans. Jayant Karve and Eleanor Zelliot. Calcutta: Seagull, 1986.

______. *Kamala*. *Silence! The Court is in Session*. *The Vultures*. *Encounter in Umbugland*. Trans. Priya Adarkar. *Sakharam Binder*. Trans. Kumud Mehta and Shanta Gokhale. *Five Plays*. Bombay: Oxford UP, 1992.

______. *Kanyadan*. Trans. Gowri Ramnarayan. Delhi: Oxford UP, 1996.

SECONDARY SOURCES

BOOKS

Barth, A. *The Religions of India.* Trans. J.Wood. Delhi: Low Price, 1982.

Bayapa Reddy, P. *The Plays of Asif Currimbhoy*. Calcutta: Writers Workshop, 1985.

______. *Studies in Indian Writing in English with a Focus on Indian English Drama*. New Delhi: Prestige, 1990.

Beauvoir, Simone de. *The Second Sex*. England: Penguin, 1972.

Berne, Eric. *Beyond Games and Scripts*. New York: Ballantine, 1983.

Bhatta, Somadeva. *King Vikram and the Ghost* (*Kathasaritsagara*). Trans. C.H. Tawney. Bombay: Jaico, 1956.

Blum, Gerald S. *Psychoanalytical Theories of Personality*. New York: McGraw, 1953.

Brown, Bruce. *Marx, Freud and the Critique of Everyday Life*. New York: Monthly Review, 1974.

Brown, Norman O. *Life against Death*. London: Routledge, 1959.

Campbell, Joseph. *The Masks of God*. 3 Vols. Harmondsworth: Penguin, 1976.

Dass, Veena Noble. *Modern Indian Drama in English Translation*. New Delhi: n.p, 1988.

Debroy, Dipavali and Bibek. *The Shiva Purana*. Delhi: Books for All, n.d.

Dhawan, R.K., ed. *Indian Literature Today*. 2 vols. 1, Delhi: Prestige, 1994.

Dr. Babasaheb Ambedkar: Writings and Speeches. Vol. 3. Bombay: Govt. of Maharashtra, 1987.

Durant, Will. *The Study of Philosophy*. New York: Pocket, 1961.

Dyer, Wayne. *The Sky's the Limit*. New York: Pocket, 1980.

Ellmann, Richard and Charles Feidelson Jr., eds. *The Modern Tradition*. New York: Oxford UP, 1965.

Freud, Sigmund. *New Introductory Lectures on Psychoanalysis*. New York: Penguin, 1977.

Fromm, Erich. *The Crisis of Psychoanalysis*. London: Jonathan Cape, 1971.

______. *The Anatomy of Human Destructiveness*. New York: Fawcett, 1975.

Fuller, B.A.G. *A History of Philosophy*. New Delhi: Oxford, 1969.

Gamst, Frederick C. and Edward Norbeck. *Ideas of Culture: Sources and Uses*. New York: Holt, 1976.

Gagri, Balwant. *Theatre in India*. New York: Theatre Arts, 1962.

George, K.M., ed. *Comparative Indian Literature*. Madras: Mac Millan, 1984.

Gowda, Anniah. *Indian Drama*. Mysore: U of Mysore, 1974.

Harris, Thomas A. *I'm OK—You're OK*. New Delhi: Sterling, 1979.

Hauser, Gayelord. *Be Happier Be Healthier*. New York: Popular Library, 1954.

Illich, Evan D. *Deschooling Society*. Harmondsworth: Penguin, 1973.

Jaya Prabha, A. *Nalugo Goda: Telugulo Adhunika Natakam 1940-1990*, (*The Fourth Wall: Modern Drama in Telugu*). Hyderabad: Charita, 1992.

Joshi, R.G. *Myth in Indian Drama*. Delhi: B.R., n.d.

Jung, C.G. *Four Archetypes*. Trans. R.F.C. Hull. London: Routledge, 1972.

Krishna Bhatta, S. *Indian English Drama: A Critical Study*. New Delhi: Sterling, 1987.

Lal, P. *The Concept of an Indian Literature*. Calcutta: Writers Workshop, 1968.

Levi, Sylvain. *The Theatre of India*. Trans. Mukherji Narayan. 2 Vols. Calcutta: Writers Workshop, 1978.

Mahle, H.S. *Indo-Anglian Fiction*. New Delhi: Jainsons, 1985.

Mann, Thomas. *The Transposed Heads*. Trans. H.T. Lowe-Porter. Calcutta: Rupa, 1961.

Marx and Engels. *Manifesto of the Communist Party*. Moscow: Progress, 1977.

Mehta, Kumud. Introduction. *Silence! The Court is in Session*. By Vijay Tendulkar. Trans. Priya Adarkar. Madras: Oxford UP, 1961.

Morris, Desmond. *The Naked Ape*. London: Corgi, 1968.

Naik, M.K. *A History of Indian English Literature*. New Delhi: Sahitya Akademi, 1982.

______. *Dimensions of Indian English Literature*. New Delhi: Sterling, 1984.

______. *Studies in Indian English Literature*. New Delhi: Sterling, 1987.

______ and S. Makashi Panekar, eds. *Perspectives on Indian Drama in English*. Madras: Oxford UP, 1977.

Pandey, Sudhakar and Freya Taraporewala, eds. *The Studies in Contemporary Indian Drama*. New Delhi: Prestige, 1990.

______. *G.B. Shaw: A Critical Response*. New Delhi: Prestige, 1992.

______. *New Directions in Indian Drama*. New Delhi: Prestige, 1994.

Porter, Thomas E. *Myth and Modern American Drama*. Ludhiana: Kalyani, 1971.

Raha, Kironmoy. *Bengali Theatre*. New Delhi: National Book Trust, 1978.

Rangacharya, Adya. *The Indian Theatre*. New Delhi: Sahitya Akademi, 1971.

Rice, Stanley. *Hindu Customs and their Origins*. Delhi: Low Price, 1993.
Roszak, Theodore. *The Making of a Counter Culture*. New York: Grove, 1957.
Schechner, Richard. *Performative Circumstances from the Avant Garde to Ramlila*. Calcutta: Seagull, 1983.
Shree Rajneesh, Bhagwan. *Get out of Your Own Way*. Poona: Rajneesh, 1977.
Singhal, D.P. *India and World Civilization*. Calcutta: Rupa, 1993.
Sircar, Badal. *The Third Theatre*. Calcutta: Sircar, 1978.
Sophocles. *The Theban Plays*. Trans. E.F. Walting. Harmondsworth: Penguin, 1974.
Srinivasa Iyengar, K.R. *Indian Writing in English*. New Delhi: Sterling, 1985.
Srinivasa Rao, Vemuri. *Poorvagathalahari*. Hyderabad: Venkatrama, 1976.
Steiner, Claude M. *Scripts People Live*. New York: Bantam, 1980.
Summerton, Oswald. *Transactional Game Analysis*. Delhi: Manohar, 1979.
Vatsyayan, Kapila. *Traditional Indian Theatre: Multiple Streams*. New Delhi: National Book Trust, 1980.
Venkata Reddy, K. *Critical Studies in Commonwealth Literature*. New Delhi: Prestige, 1994.
Wilkins, W.J. *Hindu Mythology*. Calcutta: Rupa, 1975.
William, Handy J. and Max Westbrook, eds. *Twentieth Century Criticism: The Major Statements*. New Delhi: Light & Life, 1976.
Williams, Raymond. *Drama: From Ibsen to Eliot*. London: Chatto, 1952.
Wuthnow, Robert et al., *Cultural Analysis*. Boston: Routledge, 1984.

Articles, Dissertations, Interviews and Introductions

Anantha Murthy, U.R. "A Note on Karnad's *Hayavadana*." *Literary Criterion*, VIII, 4 (1978).
______. Introduction. *Tughlaq*. By Girish Karnad. Delhi: Oxford UP, 1987. vii-x.
Arora, Keval. "The Theatre in Translation." *Humanities Review*, 2.2 (1980).
Bandyopadhyay, Samik. Introduction. *Ghashiram Kotwal* by Vijay Tendulkar. Trans. Jayant Karve and Eleanor Zelliot. Calcutta: Seagull, 1986. iii-ix.
______. Introduction. *Beyond the Land of Hattamala* and *Scandal in Fairyland* by Badal Sircar. Calcutta: Seagull, 1992. vii-ix.
Banerjee, Arundhati. Introduction. *Five Plays* by Vijay Tendulkar. Bombay: Oxford UP, 1992.
Bhaskaran, Gautaman. "Whiter English Theatre?" *The Hindu*, 25 Nov. 1990, Weekly ed. 3:1.
Bhattacharjee, Shampa. "Badal Sircar's Street Plays: A Thematic Study." Diss. Kakatiya U, 1994.
Boal, Augusto. Interview. *Seagull Theatre Quarterly*, Apr. 1994.
Chakravartee, Moutushi. "Myth and Symbol as Metaphor: A Reconstruction of *Red Oleanders* and *Hayavadana*." *Literary Criterion*, 26.4 (1991).
Coppala, Carlo. Foreword. *A Journal of South Asian Literature*, XIV. 3-4 (1979), 89-90.
Dharwadker, Aparna. "Historical Fictions and Postcolonial Representation: Reading Girish Karnad's *Tughlaq*." *PMLA*, 110.1 (1995), 43-58.
Drego, Pearl. "Ego State Models." *Tasi Darshan*, 1.4 (1981), 119-45.
______. "Parenting in Social Process." *Tasi Darshan*, 13.1 (1993), 15-25.
Dubey, Satyadev and Vijay Tendulkar. "Dialogue." *Gentleman*, Sept. 83.
Dutta, Ella. Introduction. *Three Plays* by Badal Sircar. Calcutta: Seagull, 1985. v-xi.
Eakambaram, N. "Validity of *Evam Indrajit*—An Indian Version of an Absurd Play." *Essays in Criticism on Indian Literature in English*. Ed. M.S. Nagarajan et al. New Delhi: S. Chand, 1991.

Eliot T.S. "The Waste Land." *The Faber Book of Modern Verse*. Ed. Michael Roberts. London: Faber, 1965. 91-104.

Gandhi, Krishna. "Hayavadana." *Enact*, 68-69 (1972), no page.

Ghosh, Abik. "Hayavadana Triad." *Enact*, 159-60 (1980), no page.

Gopalie, S. "Playwright in Perspective." *Enact*, 54 (1971), no page.

Gowda, Anniah H.H. "Karnad's *Tughlaq* and Ramanujan's Relation." *The Literary Half Yearly* XIV. 1 (1973).

______. "Indian Theatre in English." *Journal of Indian Writing in English* V. 1 (1977).

Guha, Naresh. "A Note on an Indian Legend in Thomas Mann." *The Image in Western Creative Writing*. Ed. M.K. Naik and S.K. Desai. Dharwar: n.p, 1971.

Hemadri, Usha. "The relevance of experimental theatre." *Indian Post*, 2 July 1989, 6.

Jaganmohan Chari, A. and E. Renuka. "The Plays of Vijay Tendulkar." *New Quest*, Jan.-Feb. 1988, 27-37.

Jain, Madhu. "Ancient Metaphors, Contemporary Messages." *India Today*, 15 March 1992, 160-61.

Jain, N.C. "Some recent significant plays." *Enact*, 25-26 (1969), no page.

______. "Rakesh, the Playwright." *Enact*, Jan.-Feb. 1973, no page.

Jha, Vivek Dutta. "Mohan Rakesh and his Plays." *Enact*, Jan.-Feb. 1973, no page.

Lal, Ananda. "From Spartcus to Quo Vadis? Bengali Theatre." *Telegraph*, 24 June 1988.

Karnad, Girish. Interview by Rajinder Paul. *Enact*, 54 (1971), no page.

______. Interview. *Indian Cinema Super Bazaar*. Ed. Aruna Vasudev and Philip Lengeet. New Delhi: Vikas, 1983. 216-28.

______. "An Integrated View of All Art Forms". *The Hindu*, 19 June 1988, 16.

______. "Is theatre dead?" *Indian Post*, 31 Dec. 1989, 6.

______. "Acrobating between the traditional and the modern." *Indian Literature*, 131 (1989), 85-99.

______. "I see myself as a playwright." *The Hindu*, 7 Oct. 1990, Weekly ed., III.

______. "Where is the tradition?" *Frontline*, 25 Sept. 1992.

______. "Theatre in India." *Daedalus*. 118.4, 330-52.

______. Author's Introduction. *Three Plays*. Delhi: Oxford UP, 1994. 1-18.

Kaur, Charanjit. "Woman's liberation and literary criticism." *New Quest* 67 (1988), 61-64.

Ketkar, Kumar. "Tendulkar's Human Zoo." *The Illustrated Weekly*, 20 Nov. 1983, 22.

Krishna Bhatta, S. "Indo-English Women Playwrights." *Triveni*, 49.1 (1980), 39-46.

______. "Indo-Anglian Drama: A Critical Study." *Triveni*, 52.3 (1983), 67-73.

______. "Epic Themes in Indo-English Plays." *Triveni*, 49.4 (1981), 43-51.

______. "Indian English Drama: Models and Technqiues." *Triveni*, 56.2 (1987), 31-35.

Kurkoti, Kirtinath. Introduction. *Hayavadana* by Girish Karnad. Delhi: Oxford UP, 1988. v-vii.

Long, Bruce J. "Life out of Death." *Hinduism*. Ed. Bardwell L. Smith. Leiden: E.J. Brill, 1982.

Maharishi, Mohan. "Changing Role of Words in Theatre: Mohan Rakesh." *Sangeet Natak*, 22 (1971), 19-27.

Marulasiddappa, K. "Drama's turning point." Trans. Chaitanya. *Spectrum*, 11 June 1994, IV.

Mazumdar, Debu. "Bengali plays look back." *The Hindustan Times*, 10 Sept. 1989, 13.

Meserve, Walter J. "Shakuntala's Daughters: Women in Contemporary Indian Drama." *World Literature Today*, 63:3 (1989), 421-25.

Nagpal, Kavita. "The Badal Sircar Magic." *The Hindustan Times*, 5 April 1992, 13.

Naik, G.H. "Karnad's *Tughlaq*." *Enact*, 193-94 (1983), no page.

Narayana, B. "Hindi Theatre: Thy Weakness is Thy Strength." *Enact*, 28 (1969), no page.

Nigam, R.L. "*Adhe Adhure*: A Comment." *Enact*, 32-33 (1969), no page.

Paul, Rajinder. "Modern Indian Theatre." *Seminar*, 359 (1989), 39-42.

______. "Karnad Plays with a Cobra." *The Book Review,* XIV. 4 (1990), 31-32.

Pramila Devi, P. "the Theatre of Violence: A Study of Vijay Tendulkar's Plays." Diss. Sri Krishnadevaraya U, 1993.

Raju, Anand Kumar. "The mind-over-body dilemma." *The Hindu*, 2 Aug. 1992, weekly ed., IV.

______. "A theatrical tour de force." *The Hindu*, 29 Nov. 1992, Weekly ed., IV.

______. "Where the end justifies the means." *The Hindu,* 21 Feb. 1993, Weekly ed., VI.

Rakesh, Mohan. "Why Plays?" *Enact,* 13-14 (1968), no page.

______. Interviews. *Enact*, 53 (1971), no page.

______. "Words and the Space Beyond." *Enact,* 66 (1972), no page.

______. "The Nehru Fellowship Project: The Dramatic Word." *Enact,* 73-74 (1973), no page.

______. "*Lehron Ke Rajhans*: Preface to the Revised Edition." *Enact*, 73-74 (1973), no page.

______. "A Self-Portrait." *A Journal of South Asian Literature,* IX, 2-3 (1973), 3-14.

______. Interview. *A Journal of South Asian Literature,* IX, 2-3 (1973), 15-39.

Ramamurthi, K.S. "Indian Drama in English with special reference to *Tughalq*." *Litt Crit,* 5.1 (1979), 9-22.

Ramnarayan, Gowri. "The Endless Road of Badal Sircar's Free Theatre." *Frontline*, 28 Aug. 1992, 73-77.

Ramanujan, A.K. "Telling Tales." *Daedalus*, 118.4, 238-61.

Renuka, E. "All about Umbugland: A Study of Vijay Tendulkar's Plays." Diss. Kakatiya U, 1984.

Samant, Nitin. "Tendulkar: A Confused Perspective," *Adhikar Raksha*. VI, 1-2 (1983).

Sastri, I. "Sircar." *Enact*, 139-40 (1978), no page.

Sarat Babu, Manchi. "Psychocultural Dynamics of Sexism." *Indian Women Novelists*. Ed. R.K. Dhawan. New Delhi: Prestige, 1993. Set II, Vol. I, 9-21.

Sethi, J.D. Rakesh's *Adhe Adhure*: A Break-Through," *Enact,* 27 (1969), no page.

Sinha, Mona. "Symposium: Importance of being Mohan Rakesh." *Enact,* 195-96 (1983), no page.

Sircar, Badal. Interview. *Enact*, 27 (1969), no page.

______. *Enact*, 59 (1971), no page.

______. Interview. *Sangeet Natak*, 22 (1971).

Sonalkar, Sudhir. "Vijay Tendulkar and the Metaphor of Violence." *The Illustrated Weekly,* 20 Nov. 1983.

Sondhi, Reeta. "*Hayavadana*: A Continuing Search." *Enact*, 204-5 (1984), no page.

Sundararaman, M.N. "Tradition and Modernity in Indian English Drama." *The Journal of Indian Writing in English*, 21.1 (1993), 1- 13.

Tapas, Vijay. "Tendulkar: The Number Two Anti-Dalit," *Adhikar Raksha*. VI, 1-2 (1983).

Thakurdas, Frank. "*Adhe Adhure*: A Comment." *Enact,* 28 (1969), no page.

Tendulkar, Vijay. Interview by Priya Adarkar. *Enact*, 49-50 (1971), no page.

______. Interview. *India Today*, 16-31 Dec. 1980.

______. *The Indian Express,* 27 March 1983, magazine sec, 5.

______. Interview. *The Week*, 8-14 May 1983.

______. "Conversation." *Onlooker,* 8-22 June 1983.

______. "I Portray Women as I see them . . ." *Femina*, 8-22 June 1984.

Venkatesan. "Caste Crimes." *Frontline,* 29 July 1994, 104.

Venkaeswarlu, K. "Badal Sircar's Third Theatre." Diss. S. K. U, 1993.

Wasi, Jehanara. "New Trail in Marathi Theatre." *Link*, 1 Oct. 1989, 36.

Index